MW01047961

READY, SET, RETIRE!

ARE YOU ON TRACK TO NAVIGATE THE
RETIREMENT MAZE?

SUZANNE M. BUSKA &
COLE J. BRUNER

This document discusses general concepts for retirement planning, and is not intended to provide tax or legal advice. Individuals are urged to consult with their tax and legal professionals regarding these issues. This handbook should ensure that clients understand a) that annuities and some of their features have costs associated with them; b) that income received from annuities is taxable; and c) that annuities used to fund IRAs do not afford any additional measure of tax deferral for the IRA owner.

Copyright © 2015 by Gradient Positioning Systems (GPS). All rights reserved. No part of this publication may be reproduced, distributed, or transmitted in any form or by any means, electronic or mechanical, including photocopying, recording, or by any information storage and retrieval system, without written permission of the publisher, except in the case of brief quotations embodied in critical reviews and certain other noncommercial uses permitted by copyright law.

Printed in the United States of America

First Printing, 2015

Gradient Positioning Systems, LLC
4105 Lexington Avenue North, Suite 110
Arden Hills, MN 55126 (877) 901-0894

Contributors: Nick Stovall, Nate Lucius, Mike Binger and Gradient Positioning Systems, LLC.

Gradient Positioning Systems, LLC, Suzanne M, Buska and Cole J. Bruner are not affiliated with or endorsed by the Social Security Administration or any government agency.

TABLE OF CONTENTS

INTRODUCTION

The year was 1939. The comic strip Superman had just debuted. Oldsmobile introduced the first car with automatic transmission, and a goldfish-swallowing craze was sweeping college campuses across the nation. Here in the city of Wausau, a young man by the name of Joseph Buska Sr. opened an independent insurance agency along the Wisconsin River and dedicated himself to selling service and solutions, and doing right by his clients.

Seventy-five years later, that tradition of service and solutions is still going strong. We are Suzanne Buska and Cole Bruner, President and Vice President—and mother and son team—at Buska Retirement Solutions, a firm specializing in personalized retirement income solutions for the people in and around Central Wisconsin. A lot of things have changed since Joseph Buska Sr. first opened his doors, but doing right by our clients has remained our mission because every day, we see evidence in our community of how a holistic approach to retirement planning contributes not just to the wealth of generations, but to their quality of life and peace of mind as well.

YOUR RETIREMENT CONCERNS

The number one fear of most retirees today is outliving their money. That kind of anxiety comes from investment products and advice that are one-sided and executed without the whole picture in mind. When are you hoping to retire? How long will your retirement last? How can you maximize your Social Security benefit and what is the best way to plan for the expense of long term care? What are the future tax issues that could affect your bottom line? The answers to these questions are complicated and depend on your individual situation. There are between 10,000 and 20,000 different filing options for Social Security benefits, countless investment and insurance products, multiple ways to structure and manage 401(k)s and IRAs for income and several options for solving long term health care needs. Your savings are only half of the retirement equation, because money by itself doesn't provide you with the security of an income that can't be outlived. It's *the plan* for putting that money to work that turns your savings into a vehicle that can take you through the retirement maze. Having a comprehensive plan you can trust takes away the fear and negative emotions so you can begin what can and should be a new and exciting phase in your life.

The concerns of the modern retiree are many, but so, too, are the available solutions. Retiring today means you need more than just savings, products and facts; you need guidance and knowledge because the world has changed since the day grandfather Buska hung his sign on the door.

SECURITY BEGINS WITH EDUCATION

Our parents and grandparents had what was arguably the best and most comfortable middle-class retirement available: a frosted cake, gold watch and a guaranteed pension that generated income for the rest of their lives. In most cases, the philosophies our parents used for their retirement years aren't going to work for us. Things have changed. In the last 12 years, we've had two significant market downturns which caused a lot of people to lose money in their retirement accounts. Many investors weren't even aware of the market risk their company savings plans were exposed to and as a result, were faced with difficult choices about reentering the work force or lowering their standard of living. *The question isn't CAN you or SHOULD you put your money to work for you and your family. It's HOW.*

The chapters that follow are designed to provide you with an education so you can learn how to evaluate your investments, how much risk they are exposed to, and how that risk relates to your timeline and the safety of your nest egg. Along the way, you'll meet hardworking people like yourself who are facing some of the same difficult challenges and decisions that you'll be making, both now and in the future. It is our intention to give you the knowledge you need to navigate those challenges in a way that protects both your independence and the retirement lifestyle you've envisioned.

Taking Control of Your Assets as outlined in Chapter Two, gives you a visual schematic to organize your assets, so you can *see* if your current investments are in alignment with your goals and participate in their restructuring. Doing this allows you to manage your risk intelligently instead of throwing money at stocks and *hoping* they go up in value. Once we get an overall view of the entire portfolio, we can then make recommendations about how to allocate a portion to safety and a portion to risk.

Risk Factors such as taxes, inflation and the rising cost of long term care have a surprisingly large impact on the amount of money you'll need to secure your retirement income. Our Retirement Analyzer reports will show you how certain events can affect the security of your income by projecting the answers to various versions of, *what happens if.* What happens to your retirement savings *if you get sick?* What happens to your lifestyle *if the stock market takes a hit?* What happens to your retirement income *if your spouse passes away?* There are new financial tools designed to address these specific concerns. Planning for all the risk factors today means building a more independent future tomorrow.

Income Planning is the heart of the retirement planning process and begins with putting together a budget of your monthly obligations. Many people haven't made the time to calculate just what their day-to-day living expenses will be during retirement, or they assume those expenses will be less. Experience shows us that the more free time we have, the more money we tend to spend. Guessing at your expenses leads to a retirement based on *I Hope So*; looking at your financial obligations, how much you need and when, turns that anxiety around so you can have a retirement based on *I Know So.*

Social Security is one guaranteed source of income that most Americans rely on, but taking this benefit at the wrong time and not understanding how to optimize other considerations such as file and suspend and spousal benefits can cost you thousands of dollars over the lifetime of your benefit. Almost half of all senior citizens file for Social Security early at the age of 62, resulting in a 25 percent reduction in benefits.* There are a few good reasons to do this, but filing because you don't know any better is not in your best interest. Running a Social Security Optimization report will tell you exactly when and how you should file to get the most out of this lifetime benefit.

When to Claim Social Security Benefits, David Blanchett, CFA, CFP January, 2013

Taxes play an ever-growing role during retirement because most people are living on a fixed income. Everyone files and pays their taxes at the end of the year, but few people know how to plan proactively for the taxes that will come due during retirement. Do you know how to structure your IRA so it can provide the most tax-advantaged benefits to you and your heirs? Taking a proactive and educated approach to taxes during your retirement can mean thousands more dollars in your pocket instead of Uncle Sam's.

The Income Gap is the difference between the guaranteed sources of income that you currently have and the income that you want to have. Filling this income gap is where alternative investment vehicles come into play. A lot of investors enter into their retirement years with 90 to 100 percent of their assets in the stock market. How do you turn those assets into a regular paycheck?

One of the biggest changes we recommend begins with reducing that risk in advance of retirement. The process of getting something guaranteed built into your portfolio is the foundation of income generation, and that requires a shift as you move out of the accumulation stage and into the preservation stage.

TOO GOOD TO BE TRUE?

Once you stop working and the paychecks stop coming in, there are no more contributions going into your retirement savings accounts. The accumulation stage of your life where you work and save those assets is about to end, and the distribution phase is about to begin. Before you start taking those dollars out, it's a good idea to consider the preservation of what you have so carefully built up. Going through the preservation stage before beginning those distributions will both secure and maximize your income sources. The trick here is that even though you are entering the preservation stage, you still want to have growth.

There are a lot of people out there who will give you advice about what to do with your money, but not all of them will have your best interest in mind. Before you trust your advisor and do what they tell you, ask yourself, *how much money are you comfortable giving away to stock market loss?* If the answer is none, this book can help educate you about the new indexed annuities designed to provide retirees with *both* growth and principal protection.

People often say that indexed annuities are too good to be true. They provide the protection of a contracted guarantee linked to market returns, and with the purchase of an income rider, you can receive regular payments during your retirement for the rest of your life. The income riders on today's indexed annuities use the power of annual reset to maintain the basis of your gains, so you won't lose this money, even if the stock market takes a dive.

This is one way you can design your own pension plan to replicate the *guaranteed for life* income enjoyed by our parents, but it's not the only way. Building a solid future means you want to have access to not just one or two investment products, but a full spectrum of solutions designed to meet your ever-changing needs.

RETIRING WITH THE BUSKA FAMILY

It was the French philosopher Alain who said that history is a grand view of the present and not simply something in the past. The history of the Buska Insurance Agency is living by that example.

When Joseph Buska Jr. took over the firm from his father, he expanded the operation to include a specialist in retirement benefits who happened to be his daughter, Suzanne. Today, Suzanne operates her own firm, Buska Retirement Solutions, which employs a fourth-generation Buska and operates as the parent company to Buska Wealth Management, LLC, a Registered Investment Advisory firm held to fiduciary standards of liability. As financial professionals, we are legally obligated to offer solutions that are in our client's best interest. To that end, we offer the following:

- Financial Planning for Individuals, Families, Corporations and Trusts*
- Comprehensive Retirement Income Planning*
- Active Wealth Management and Monitoring*
- Guaranteed Lifetime Income Options**
- 401(k) and IRA Rollovers
- Asset Protection and Distribution
- Social Security Optimization
- Final Expense Planning
- Long-Term Care Solutions
- Wealth Transfer Strategies
- Survivorship Planning
- Mortgage Services

As an independent insurance firm, we are able to utilize dozens of insurance carriers to find the best rates and products to fit your specific needs. We also offer professional money management through our strategic alliance with Gradient Investments, LLC (GI), an SEC-Registered Investment Advisor firm offering clients over twenty proprietary portfolios. The portfolios are managed by their Chief Investment Officer, Wayne Schmidt, CFA, MBA and Sr. Portfolio Manager, Michael Binger, CFA.

During your retirement years, the financial decisions you make impact not just your life, but the life of your spouse, loved one and family members for years to come. Working with us here at Buska, you join our family, adding to the growing number

---

*Investment advisory services offered through Buska Wealth Management, LLC, a Registered Investment Advisor in the state of Wisconsin. Insurance products and services offered through Buska Retirement Solutions, Inc. Buska Wealth Management, LLC and Buska Retirement Solutions, Inc. are affiliated companies.
**Based on claims paying ability of issuing carrier.

of individuals just like you who deserve the peace of mind that comes from planning the retirement you deserve.

— *Suzanne Buska, President of Buska Retirement Solutions, Inc. and Licensed Insurance Professional.*

— *Cole Bruner, Vice President at Buska Retirement Solutions as well as President and Investment Advisor Representative for the Registered Investment Advisory firm, Buska Wealth Management, LLC.*

1

GETTING TO KNOW YOU

Will we have enough money for retirement?

George and Dee Weston raised their three boys, Sam, Nathan and Edward, in their split-level home along the Wisconsin River. George worked 30 years at a manufacturing plant, and Dee worked as a dental hygienist. When they both retired at the age of 65, all three of their boys had finished college, were married and building lives of their own. Both George and Dee had made regular contributions to their company 401(k) plans but they didn't really know how to convert those investments into a monthly income stream. In order to help pay for their sons' college education, they had taken a second mortgage out, so they were still making house payments.

They hoped they had saved enough money to cover their expenses during retirement, but they didn't know for sure.

THE WESTON FAMILY TREE

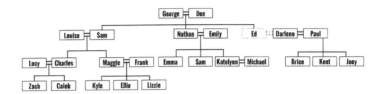

The "Weston family" is a fictitious family used as an example to demonstrate retirement concepts only. Any resemblance to persons living or deceased is purely coincidental.

At age 65, both George and Dee were eligible for Social Security, so they filed right away without looking at their options. Once their checks started coming in, they realized they needed more money than they thought they did in order to meet their monthly obligations. To make ends meet, George starting tapping into their 401(k)s.

A year after making withdrawals, Dee started to get worried. Both her parents had lived well into their mid-eighties, and George's mother was still alive at the age of 92. She had relocated to a nursing home after her husband passed away, and suddenly Dee found herself wondering what would happen to her if George passed away. She didn't know anything about their investments or how to make withdrawals on her 401(k). She also started hearing disturbing reports on the news about the global economy and stock market predictions.

Another year went by and when George and Dee looked at the account balances on their 401(k), they saw that their savings were dwindling away. Dee wasn't able to sleep at night because here she was only 67 and they had already started dipping into their principal. How would their nest egg last them for the next twenty or thirty years? Dee didn't know. She told George one morning over coffee, "I can't take this anymore. We have to get some answers." George and Dee made an appointment with a financial professional.

After meeting with the couple and learning about their situation, their financial professional showed them how they were positioned for risk. Their number one fear was running out of money, yet nearly 100 percent of their nest egg was linked to stock market investments that weren't even generating income from dividend returns. They had done nothing to secure the safety of the money they were relying on to pay the bills, and nothing to plan for the realities of what could be coming down the road.

With the help of their financial professional, they restructured their assets into an income-driven portfolio. Once their money was reallocated, they were able to meet their monthly obligations from regular annuity payments and dividend interest, without dipping at all into their principal. They also made provisions for income continuation should one of them pass away. Now, their account value is no longer going down every year. Now, George and Dee know they have enough money for retirement.

While George and Dee might sound like they're totally in the dark about their retirement, the truth is there are a lot of people just like them. They know retirement is coming and they know they have some assets to rely on, but they aren't sure how it will all come together to provide them with a retirement income.

You spend your entire working life hoping what you put into your retirement accounts will help you live comfortably once you clock out of the workforce for good. The key word in that sentiment and the word that can make retirement feel like a looming problem instead of a rewarding life stage, is **hope**. You hope you'll have enough money.

Leaving your retirement up to chance is unadvisable by nearly any standard, yet millions of people find themselves *hoping* instead of planning for a happy ending. **Most people spend more** *time planning their vacations than they spend planning for their retirement.* Like George and Dee, they have spent a lifetime working and earning money, and now they just want to relax and enjoy that money. What they find, however, is that peace of mind simply isn't possible without a plan.

Most retirees discover that if they take the time to move through the planning phase and answer a few important questions about their goals, needs and wants, not only can they achieve stability of income they need, they can also achieve the retirement of their dreams. How is this possible? By taking the *hope* out your retirement and replacing it with the knowledge that comes from having a solid plan.

WHERE ARE YOU AT?

Your lifestyle, your desires, and your idea of how you want to live are all factors that will shape the way you structure your investments to deliver the retirement you want. Getting a handle on your retirement and creating a plan that draws on the strength of diversity and security begins not with the investments, but with the goals of you, the investor. A financial professional held to fiduciary standards will seek first to understand where you are before advising you on products and tools. He or she will be looking past the numbers to the people and events that matter most to you, because your income plan must be designed to meet your goals. The right investment tools can help you achieve those goals, taking you from where you are at now to the future you choose.

To build anything you need to have three things: a plan, a process, and the help of a professional.

During your first meeting with your financial professional, he or she will begin the process by asking questions designed to get to know you better. Questions about you, your life and your family members can include the following:

- What situation are you currently in?

- Who are you living with?
- Are you married or divorced?
- Do you have any children?
- When do you want to retire?
- How is your health?
- Do you have any concerns or worries about your current financial situation?
- What do you need during your retirement in order to be happy?

From there, questions will turn more specifically to your investments. Expect questions such as:
- Where is your portfolio?
- How is the money within your portfolio allocated?
- Will you be receiving a pension?
- Do you have other sources of income during retirement such as rental income?
- Do you have life insurance?

Planning for retirement isn't just about the numbers. It's about the people important to you, and the things you hold dear. The job of the financial professional is to help you get the most out of every dollar you have saved so you can take care of what's important. When deciding on whether or not an investment is a good fit for a retiree, these are the core considerations that can help a professional determine which investment tools are in your best interest.

Be aware, however, that not all financial professionals have your best interests at heart. There are many designations that a financial professional can earn during their career. When looking for a financial professional you can trust, you want to work with someone obligated to act in good faith and in the best interests of their clients.

WHO ARE YOU WORKING WITH?
BOOTS VS. SNEAKERS

It can be hard to know who to trust these days when it comes to advice about money. While no one cares more about your money than you do, when looking for advice and guidance about the structuring of your retirement assets, it's important to understand the legal standards your financial professional is held to. The motivation behind the advice given can be best understood by looking at the difference between suitability and fiduciary standards.

Suitability standards dictate that your financial professional can sell you a product as long as it can be considered suitable, even though the product might not necessarily be the best fit for your needs.

To help illustrate this point, let's say that you are living in Wisconsin, getting ready for the winter, and you need to secure footwear protection. If you went to a professional held to suitability standards, they could recommend a pair of sneakers as "suitable" protection for your feet, even though sneakers are a far cry from what you need. A professional held to suitability standards might make this recommendation because in selling you those sneakers, he or she receives the highest commission. You could walk away from this encounter having spent a good deal of money on a product not in your best interest, and your feet would suffer.

In terms of your retirement, this can be compared to investments products that might be considered "suitable," although they are not the best choices for income generation. It's easy to know when you've made the wrong choice with regards to footwear; with investment products, however, your mistakes might not show up as quickly. This is where fiduciary standards come in to play.

Operating under fiduciary standards, financial professionals are obligated to act in good faith and with candor, to be proactive in disclosing any conflicts of interest that may

impact a client, and to make recommendations that are always in the client's best interest.

The National Association of Personal Financial Advisors (NAPFA) describes financial professionals held to fiduciary standards as occupying a position of special trust and confidence when working with a client, because they are required to act with undivided loyalty.* This includes disclosure of how the financial advisor is to be compensated and any corresponding conflicts of interest.

If you went to a professional held to fiduciary standards and told them you needed something to protect your feet, they would ask you several questions first before recommending any shoes, questions such as: What are you hoping these shoes will do for you? When will you be needing these shoes? Where is it you hope these shoes will take you? After learning that you want foot protection to withstand a sub-zero winter filled with piles of snow, this professional would be legally obligated to help you find the best pair of boots out there with your budget in mind. This is why *getting to know you* is such an important part of the planning process when working with a fiduciary professional.

Another factor that influences the kinds of investment products and tools a professional might recommend has to do with the products that are available to them. No matter how good a financial professional is, the firm that they represent needs to operate on principles that make sense in today's economy. An independent firm is not limited to certain brand names, strategies or products. Instead, they have access to the best of all available options. Using our footwear analogy, an independent firm will be educated about, and have access to, every kind of shoe out there, from boots that can withstand 40 below to sandals designed to cool your toes. They consider the newest materials being used in

---

*http://www.napfa.org/about/FiduciaryOath.asp

their industry such as polar fleece, thermal insulation and Velcro closures that improve durability and function, and they would recommend these products if they were in your best interest. The newest footwear designs can be compared to today's newer investment products such as indexed annuities and life insurance products.

Ask yourself, do you want to work with a professional who recommends investment products and strategies that are in your best interest, or theirs? What's at stake here is more than a few blisters or frozen toes. The security of your retirement income depends on it. Independent professionals held to fiduciary standards strive to break free from old ways of thinking by providing clients with products, services and strategies that make sense in today's times.

ADVICE FOR TODAY'S RETIREMENT

Even if you spend a lifetime saving and doing the right things, choosing the wrong investments during the years just prior to and immediately after retirement can prove detrimental to the longevity of your income. Fewer and fewer people are retiring with pensions like their parents did and more and more of us have to rely on our savings to produce income. Old rules and advice followed by our parents about how to invest our savings are simply not advisable in today's times. For one thing, retirement spans across more years than it used to. Many retirees like George and Dee are worried about outliving their savings, and this is a real concern given today's longer life expectancy. Today's seniors can expect to live longer than their parents did—19 years longer for men and 15 years longer for women according to the Social Security Administration.*

---

http://www.ncbi.nlm.nih.gov/books/NBK62373/

Annual withdrawal rates have also been changing. The annual withdrawal rate is the percent of money you safely take out from your nest egg every year without depletion of your funds. Longevity, market volatility and the average return rate all affect withdrawal rate. We are living in an economic environment that projects lower return rates than what we've seen in the past, which means a realistic plan must take that into account. During the 1990s when the average return rate was higher than it is now, the annual withdrawal rate that was considered safe was about 5 percent. Today, the Wall Street Journal sets the safe withdrawal rate at only 2 percent. Following this model means you would need a much larger stock market portfolio in order to avoid tapping into your principal. But what percent of your portfolio should be invested in stock market investments?

The ten-year period prior to and the years just after retiring are especially crucial to the health and viability of your portfolio, because a loss during this time can significantly reduce the ability of your savings to last for the long term. The many retirees who lost a good portion of their retirement money during the 2008 market correction had to drastically rethink their plans. Many were forced to go back to work and wait another eight years for the market to recover or risk running out of money. You don't have to put your future retirement at risk. You can choose instead to rethink how you look at your savings, because during retirement, the purpose of your money changes. **Maintaining a comfortable lifestyle during retirement depends on one thing: the ability of your savings to generate a comfortable income**. During your working years, the job of your savings was to accumulate and grow. Because your focus up to this point has been on accumulating and stockpiling money, it's hard to understand that higher annual average yields and bigger returns no longer matter. What matters is the ability of an investment to produce income. When looking at your money this way, you'll see there are two kinds of investments: I Hope So and I Know So.

I HOPE SO OR I KNOW SO: THE IMPORTANCE OF A PLAN

Retirees looking to rethink how their assets are positioned can look at their investment in terms of I *Hope So* and I *Know So*. Everyone can divide their money into these two categories. Some have more of one kind than the other. The goal may not be to eliminate one kind of money but rather to balance them so they reflect your income needs and risk tolerance as you approach retirement.

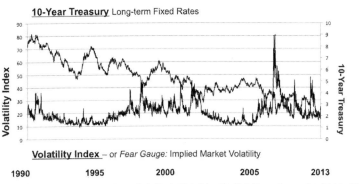

10-Year Treasury Long-term Fixed Rates

Volatility Index – or *Fear Gauge:* Implied Market Volatility

1990　　1995　　2000　　2005　　2013

Source: Yahoo Finance – 12-31-2013. VIX is a trademarked ticker symbol for the Chicago Board Options Exchange Market Volatility Index, a popular measure of the implied volatility of S&P 500 index options. Often referred to as the fear index or the fear gauge, it represents one measure of the market's expectation of stock market volatility over the next 30 day period. (wikipedia.com) The CBOE 10-year Treasury Note (TNX) is based on 10 times the yield-to-maturity on the most recently auctioned 10-year Treasury note. Past performance does not guarantee future results. Some illustrations may show how a market index has performed. An investor cannot invest in an index, although there are some investments designed to mirror index performance. Past performance is not a guarantee of future results.

The VIX, or volatility index, of the market represents expected market volatility. When the VIX drops, economic experts expect less volatility. When the VIX rises, more volatility is expected.

1. *VIX is a trademarked ticker symbol for the Chicago Board Options Exchange (CBOE) Market Volatility Index, a popular measure of the implied volatility of S&P 500 index options. Often referred to as the fear index or the fear gauge, it represents one measure of the market's expectation of stock market volatility over the next 30 day period. (wikipedia.com)*

2. *The CBOE 10-Year Treasury Note (TNX) is based on 10 times the yield-to-maturity on the most recently auctioned 10-year Treasury note.*

I Hope So Money is money that is at risk. It fluctuates with the market. It has no minimum guarantee. It is subject to investor activity, stock prices, market trends, buying trends, etc. You get the picture. This money is exposed to more risk but also has the potential for more reward. Because the market is subject to change, you can't really be sure what the value of your investments will be worth in the future. You can't really *rely* on it at all. For this reason, we refer to it as I Hope So Money. This doesn't mean you shouldn't have some money invested in the market, but it would be dangerous to assume you can know what it will be worth in the future.

I Hope So Money can be one element of a retirement plan, especially in the early stages of planning when you can trade volatility for potential returns, and when a longer investment timeframe is available to you. In the long run, time can smooth out the ups and downs of money exposed to the market. Working with a professional and leveraging a long-term investment strategy has the potential to create rewarding returns from I Hope So Money.

I Know So Money, on the other hand, is safer when compared to I Hope So Money. I Know So Money is made up of dependable, low-risk or no-risk money, and investments that you can count on. Social Security is one of the most common forms of I Know So Money. Income you draw or will draw from Social Security is guaranteed. You have paid into Social Security your entire career, and you can rely on that money during your retirement. Unlike the market, rates of growth for I Know So Money are dependent on 10-year treasury rates. The 10-year treasury, or TNX, is commonly considered to represent a very secure and safe place for your money, hence I Know So Money. The 10-year treasury drives key rates for things such as mortgage rates or CD rates. I Know So Money may not be as exciting as I Hope So Money, but it is safer. You can safely be fairly sure you will have it in the future.

Ideally, the rates of return on I Hope So and I Know So Money would have an overlapping area that provided an acceptable rate of risk for both types of money. In the early 1990s, interest rates were high and market volatility was low. At that time, you could invest in either I Hope So or I Know So Money options because the rates of return were similar from both I Know So and I Hope So investments, and you were likely to be fairly successful with a wide range of investment options. At that time, you could expose yourself to an acceptable amount of risk or an acceptable fixed rate. Basically, it was difficult to make a mistake during that time period. Today, you don't have those options. Market volatility is at all-time highs while interest rates are at all-time lows. They are so far apart from each other that it is hard to know what to do with your money.

As we stated earlier, yesterday's investment rules may not work today. Not only could they hamper achieving your goals, they may actually harm your financial situation. We are currently in a period when the rates for I Know So Money options are at historic lows, and the volatility of I Hope So Money is higher than ever. There is no overlapping acceptable rate, making both options less than ideal. *Because of this uncertain financial landscape, wise investment strategies are more important now than ever.*

This unique situation requires fresh ideas and investment tools that haven't been relied on in the past. Investing the way your parents did will not pay off. The majority of investment ideas used by financial professionals in the 1990s aren't applicable to today's markets. That kind of investing will likely get you in trouble and compromise your retirement. Today, you need a better PLAN.

HOW MUCH RISK ARE YOU EXPOSED TO?

Many investors don't know how much risk they are exposed to. It is helpful to organize your assets so you can have a clear understanding of how much of your money is at risk and how much is in safer holdings. This process starts with listing all of your assets. Let's take a look at the two kinds of money:

I Hope So Money is, as the name indicates, money that you *hope* will be there when you need it. I Hope So Money represents what you would like to get out of your investments. Examples of I Hope So Money include:

- Stock market funds, including index funds
- Mutual funds
- Variable annuities
- REITS
- Bonds

I Know So Money is money that you know you can count on. It is safer money that isn't exposed to the level of volatility as the asset types noted above. You can more confidently count on having this money when you need it. Examples of I Know So Money are:

- Savings and checking accounts
- Fixed indexed annuities
- CDs
- Money market accounts

» *Ed is the youngest son of George and Dee Weston. He moved to Chicago, worked as a tax accountant for a large banking firm, and married Darlene. He participated in the 401(k) plan offered through his employer and put in the maximum amount each year. A few years ago, Ed changed jobs so he and his wife could live outside of the city. When Ed set up a new retirement account, he transferred all the money from his old 401(k) into a new one, and that got him looking at his statements. Ed is now 55 years old and about ten years away from retirement, but he realizes that nearly every dollar he has saved for retirement is subject to market risk.*

Ed talks to a broker about his investments, and the broker tells him, "Oh, you're ten years away from retirement. There's no need to worry about that now." But Ed still feels uneasy. Several of his parents' friends lost 40 percent or more of their retirement savings during the market downturn of 2008, and some of them had to drastically alter their retirement plans.

Intuitively, Ed knows that the time has come to shift some assets to an investment alternative that is safer, but how much is the right amount?

INTRODUCING THE RULE OF 100

Determining the amount of risk that is right for you is dependent on a number of variables. You need to feel comfortable with where and how you are investing your money, and your financial professional is obligated to help you make decisions that put your money in places that fit your risk criteria.

While there is no single approach to investment risk that is universally applicable to everyone, there are some helpful guidelines. One of the most useful is called *The Rule of 100*.

The average investor needs to accumulate assets to create a retirement plan that provides income during retirement and also allows for legacy planning. To accomplish this, they need to balance the amount of risk to which they are exposed. Risk is required because, while I Know So Money is safer, more reliable and more dependable, it doesn't grow very fast, if at all. Today's historically low interest rates barely break even with current inflation. I Hope So Money, while less dependable, has more potential for growth. I Hope So Money can eventually become I Know So Money once you move it to an investment with lower risk. Everyone's risk diversification will be different depending on their goals, age and their existing assets.

So how do you decide how much risk your assets should be exposed to? Where do you begin? Luckily, there's a guideline you can use to start making decisions about risk management. It's called the Rule of 100.

WHAT IS YOUR RISK NUMBER?

The Rule of 100 is a general rule that helps shape asset diversification* for the average investor. The rule states that the number 100 minus an investor's age equals the amount of assets they should have exposed to risk.

> **The Rule of 100**: 100 - (your age) = the percentage of your assets that should be exposed to risk (I Hope So Money)

For example, if you are a 30-year-old investor, the Rule of 100 would indicate that you should be focusing on investing primarily in the market and taking on a substantial amount of risk in your portfolio. The Rule of 100 suggests that 70 percent of your investments should be exposed to risk.

100 - (30 years of age) = 70 percent

Now, not every 30-year-old should have exactly 70 percent of their assets in mutual funds and stocks. The Rule of 100 is based on

Asset Diversification disclosure – Diversification and asset allocation does not assure or guarantee better performance and cannot eliminate the risk of investment loss. Before investing, you should carefully read the applicable volatility disclosure for each of the underlying funds, which can be found in the current prospectus.

your chronological age, not your "financial age," which could vary based on your investment experience, your aversion or acceptance of risk and other factors. While this rule isn't an ironclad solution to anyone's finances, it's a pretty good place to start. Once you've taken the time to look at your assets with a professional to determine your risk exposure, you can use the Rule of 100 to make changes that put you in a more stable investment position — one that reflects your comfort level.

Perhaps when you were age 30 and starting your career, like in the example above, it made sense to have 70 percent of your money in the market: you had time on your side. You had plenty of time to save more money, work more and recover from a downturn in the market. Retirement was ages away, and your earning power was increasing. And indeed, younger investors should take on more risk for exactly those reasons. The potential reward of long-term involvement in the market outweighs the risk of investing when you are young.

Risk tolerance generally reduces as you get older, however. If you are 40 years old and lose 30 percent of your portfolio in a market downturn this year, you have 20 or 30 years to recover it. If you are 68 years old, you have five to 10 years (or less) to make the same recovery. That new circumstance changes your whole retirement perspective. At age 68, it's likely that you simply aren't as interested in suffering through a tough stock market. There is less time to recover from downturns, and the stakes are higher. The money you have saved is money you will soon need to provide you with income, or is money that you already need to meet your income demands.

Much of the flexibility that comes with investing earlier in life is related to *compounding*. Compounded earnings can be incredibly powerful over time. The longer your money has time to compound, the greater your wealth will be. This is what most people talk about when they refer to putting their money to work. This is also why the Rule of 100 favors risk for the young. If you start investing when you are young, you can invest smaller amounts of money in a more aggressive fashion because you have the potential to make a profit in a rising market and you can harness the power of compounding earnings. When you are 40, 50 or 60 years old, that potential becomes less and less and you are forced to have more money at lower amounts of risk to realize the same returns. **It basically becomes more expensive to prudently invest the older you get.**

You risk not having a recovery period the older you get, so should have fewer of your assets at risk in volatile investments. You should shift with the Rule of 100 to protect your assets and ensure that they will provide you with the income you need in retirement. Let's look at another example that illustrates how the Rule of 100 becomes more critical as you age. An 80-year-old investor who is retired and is relying on retirement assets for income, for example, needs to depend on a solid amount of I Know So Money. The Rule of 100 says an 80-year-old investor should have a maximum of 20 percent of his or her assets at risk. Depending on the investor's financial position, even less risk exposure may be required. You are the only person who can make this kind of determination, but the Rule of 100 can help. Everyone has their own level of comfort. Your Rule of 100 results will be based on your values and attitudes as well as your comfort with risk. A financial professional can look at your assets with you and discuss alternatives to optimize your balance between I Know So and I Hope So Money.

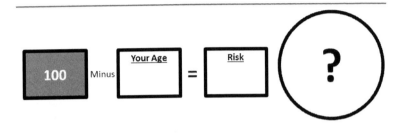

CHAPTER 1 RECAP //

- Having a planful approach to retirement begins with the individual concerns of you, the retiree. What do you want to be doing during your retirement? Who do you want to be doing those things with? This should be the time in your life when your money goes to work for you.

- Understand the source of the investment advice you are given. A professional held to fiduciary standards is legally bound to recommend products that are in your best interest. A professional held to suitability standards is not prohibited from recommending products that pay out the highest fees to him or her, as long as those products are "suitable." Suitability isn't wrong; it just may not be the best fit for retirees.

- The rules for retirement planning have changed. Today's withdrawal rates are much lower than they used to be, and most retirees are living longer than their parents did. Retirees today must look at their investments in terms of the income they can produce and NOT in terms of their returns.

- Understanding where and how your assets are invested is key to securing the safety of your income. There is money you hope you'll have in the future, and there's money you know you'll have in the future. With the help of a financial professional, it's easy to see what percentages of your assets are invested in risk, I Hope So Money, and safe, I Know So Money.

- Use the Rule of 100 as a general guiding principle when determining how much risk your retirement investments should be exposed to (100 - [your age] = [percentage of your investments that can comfortably be exposed to risk]).

2

TAKING CONTROL OF YOUR ASSETS

Where should I invest my money?

George and Dee's middle son, Nathan, married a nice girl from North Dakota who inherited some land. When Nathan's wife, Emily, was diagnosed with MS at the age of 33, the couple decided they wanted to make an investment that would take care of their three children, Katelynn, Emma and Sam. They wanted this investment to be safe and guaranteed, so the money could help pay for their college educations, help them out when they started their own families, bought homes or opened a business. Emily sold the mineral rights to her land for $1.2 million dollars and invested the proceeds in an account the couple earmarked for their kids.

Seven years later, Nathan and Emily were visiting George and Dee for a family reunion. Dee seemed happy and was talking about a wonderful picnic she had been to, hosted by her financial professional's firm. "They really care about their clients. They even cooked all the food!"

At the end of the day, Emily asked Dee if she could give her a referral. "I need to learn more about my investments," she told Dee. "I want to make sure they can help take care of my children when I no longer can."

Nathan and Emily went in to talk to Dee's financial professional, and she asked them, "What do you want this investment to do for you?" They explained the purpose of the money and told her they wanted to make sure the money was safe and guaranteed. After looking over their statements, the professional saw that Nathan and Emily were invested in two different variable annuities that took up all of their $1.2 million in assets. "Well," she told them, "For one thing, these investments are neither safe nor guaranteed."

The variable annuities had never been explained to the couple, and neither Nathan nor Emily knew how they worked, what risk they were exposed to, or what they were paying in fees. After walking them through the terms of the investment, the professional called both companies to find out about all the built-in fees. Over the seven-year period that Emily and Nathan had held the investment, they learned they had paid out more than $300,000 in fees. This was money they would never get back, and money that would never go to their children.

In our first meeting, we learn about you, your life, and what assets you have. In our second meeting, we take a look at what those investments are actually doing for you in terms of risk, reward and cost. Many investors like Emily and Nathan are surprised to find that they don't have what they think they had. When you look at your investments in terms of whether or not they align with your goals, you might realize that changes need to be made.

In thinking about your investments in terms of income production during retirement, you may also find that you have a different level of risk tolerance than you did during your working years, when growth and accumulation were your main focus. *Separating your money into different accounts depending on the purpose of the money is one way to help you gain clarity about risk.*

The money that you rely on for income must come from investments that provide you with principal guarantees. Money needed for income should have minimal exposure to the risk of loss because you don't have enough time to wait and let the money grow again. You must know with a degree of certainty that the money will be there in order to meet your monthly obligations. Before you begin taking money out of your investments to pay the bills, you want to transition into *the preservation stage* in order to secure and maximize the sources of your income. You want to take the savings you have so carefully built up, and you want to protect them. Any money left over after your income needs have been met can then be put into a separate account marked for more aggressive growth. If those investments are in the stock market, a loss will not affect your ability to meet your monthly obligations, and any profit can be used for supplemental income to fund luxuries such as fun trips or more extensive travel.

THE COLORS OF YOUR INVESTMENTS

Some investment products are better suited for income production while other vehicles are more suited for short or long term growth. Still other products are designed to provide income, guarantees *and* growth. To help you decide which investments are the right choices for your retirement goals, it can be helpful to assign colors according to the amount of risk the investment is exposed to.

For our purposes, I Know So Money (which is safer and more dependable) is green. I Hope So Money (which is exposed to risk and fluctuates with the market) is red. Yellow money is Red Money that is being actively managed. It has risk associated with it, but because this money is under the watchful eye of a professional, that risk is mitigated. The professional managing your money should know not just about the investments, but about you—what you need the money for and how you expect the investment to perform. A financial professional can help you better understand the color of the money in your investment portfolio.

When using the Rule of 100 to calculate your level of risk, your financial age might be different than your chronological age. The way you organize your assets depends on your goals and your level of comfort with risk. Whatever you determine the appropriate amount of risk for you to be, you will need to organize your portfolio to reflect your goals. If you have more Red Money than Green Money, in particular, you will need to make decisions about how to move it. You can work with a financial professional to find appropriate Green Money options for your situation.

The next step is to know the right amount and ratio of Green and Red Money for you at your stage of retirement planning.

Green Money	Red Money
"Green Money" is safer.	"Red Money" is at risk.
This is money that offers a minimum guarantee but it may pose risks other than market risk.	This is money that can go up or down in value. It may pose risk if it is not properly managed to serve a specific purpose in a comprehensive plan.

Investing heavily in Red Money and gambling all of your assets on the market is incredibly risky no matter where you fall within the Rule of 100. Money in the market can't be depended on to generate income, and a plan that leans too heavily on Red Money can easily fail, especially when investment decisions are influenced by emotional reactions to market downturns and recoveries. Not only is this an unwise plan, it can be incredibly stressful to an investor who is gambling everything on stocks and mutual funds.

But a plan that uses too much Green Money and avoids all volatility can also fail. Why? Investing all of your money in Certificates of Deposit (CDs), savings accounts, money markets and other low return accounts may provide interest and income, but that likely won't be enough to keep pace with inflation. If you focus exclusively on income from Green Money and avoid owning any stocks or mutual funds in your portfolio, you won't be able to leverage the potential for long-term growth your portfolio needs to stay healthy and productive. This is where the Rule of 100 can help you determine how much of your money should be invested in the market to anticipate your future needs. A conversation with your financial professional can also help you determine what percentage of your money should be invested in Red, Green, or Yellow Money investments. Finding the right investment tool for the job during today's economy often means utilizing multiple investment products, which is why many professionals held to fiduciary standards rely on in-depth reports and tests in order to get an objective view of your current investments.

WHAT WOULD HAPPEN IF?

There are several reports or tests a financial professional can run for you in order to help assess the performance of your current investments. The Portfolio Analysis Review (also known as PAR) uses sophisticated computer algorithm programs to reveal how your assets are currently allocated and how their performance compares with select indices in terms of both return and yield. The Social Security Optimization report runs through all the thousands of different filing combinations and tells you exactly what month and year to claim your benefit for the maximum lifetime amount of money. The Retirement Analyzer shows you what could happen to your retirement income if certain life events took place.

Risk is about more than just where your money is invested. It's about planning for the realities coming down the road. We call these realities *what if* scenarios. The Retirement Analyzer can show you how these real-life "what if" events would impact your retirement plans. If the impact is something that you are not comfortable with, then your financial professional can make the appropriate recommendations to alleviate the concern.

What would happen to your retirement income if the stock market took a loss? Based on your portfolio's current allocation, if the market took a plunge like the one endured by retirees in 2008, what would happen to your income? Would it stay the same, or would it go down? Would you have to adjust your withdrawal rate? Would you be in danger of running out of money down the road? Separating your investments according to what you want the money to do for you is one way to protect yourself against market loss. If you need $3,000 a month to pay the mortgage, put food on your table and gas in the car, then you want to protect the principal that will be supplying you with that income. There are investment tools and products that can give you guaranteed protection while also providing enough to growth to keep up with inflation.

What would happen to your retirement income if your spouse passed away? Some retirees count on one or more pensions received by a spouse. With traditional defined-benefit plans, the income goes away when the person passes away, which means a retiree loses more than just their spouse, they lose their ability to make ends meet. Social Security is another type of defined benefit plan that ends once a person is deceased. Spousal benefits give you the option to choosing the larger of the two benefit amounts should your spouse pass away, but still, you will only be getting one check, when before you were getting two. How would this affect your bottom line? If your spouse passed away tomorrow, would your income stay the same, or would it go down? What sources of income would you no longer receive? Do you have other investments such as a life insurance policy that would go into effect? There are spousal continuation options for most defined benefit plans, and today's indexed annuities give you the ability to define your own income stream with joint income options. This means you can choose an investment vehicle that will guarantee your income in the event of spousal death.

While this is undeniably an unpleasant subject to think about, not planning for spousal continuation often results in irreversible money mistakes. Losing someone you care about is never easy. When you combine that emotional toll with financial stress, you end up making mistakes that can have a devastating impact on the ability of your savings to last for the long haul.

What would happen to your retirement savings if you got sick? Health care expenses and the financial effects of chronic illness are a growing concern for today's retirees, and for good reason. The Congressional Budget Office reported in 2004 that seniors in general are not prepared for the costs of long term care, citing an annual cost of $66,000 annually for a private room in a nursing home.* More recent figures for long term nursing home stays in the State of Wisconsin put numbers between $86,505 - $102,049 annually, according to the U.S. Department of Health and Human Services.**

---

http://www.cbo.gov/publication/15584
**http://longtermcare.gov/costs-how-to-pay/costs-of-care-in-your-state/*

How long will you need this care? Women have been shown to need care longer than men, on average of 3.7 years, but numbers vary based on the age of your admission.* One thing that doesn't seem to vary is the number of retirees who don't want to think about getting sick. According to a 2010 Gallup poll, 76 percent of Americans don't believe they will ever need long term care, yet according to a 2008 Government Accountability Office (GOA) report, **married couples over the age of 65 have an 80 percent chance that at least one of them will at some time require nursing home services or long term care.**

Most people make the mistake of thinking they have to be sick in order to need long term care. This is not always the case. As we age, it becomes increasingly difficult to perform simple daily tasks. Menial custodial chores such as taking out the garbage, shopping for food, and other necessities can get harder to do, especially when living alone or with a chronic illness. A person hired for this type of home care performs activities such as driving and shopping for groceries; they can also assist with bathing, cooking, and housekeeping. Home health care providers, on the other hand, are qualified to dispense medical care and advice. In the state of Wisconsin, the current average for home care that includes personal care and homemaker services costs $20 to $22 dollars an hour for an annual average high of $49,192.**

While this may be an unpleasant subject to think about, without planning, it's quite possible that today's retirees could lose more of their retirement savings due to the costs of long term care than even the harshest of stock market downturns. Planning for this reality not only helps preserve your assets, it is one way you can control what happens to you.

---

*http://longtermcare.gov/the-basics/how-much-care-will-you-need/
**http://www.ltcoptions.com/long-term-care-wisconsin/cost-of-care/

» *Nathan and Emily are starting to think about their retirement. Nathan's wife, Emily, is not in very good health. She was diagnosed with MS in her 30s, and as a result, she is not in good shape. At some point, Nathan realizes his wife may become wheelchair-bound, and he wants to make sure that Emily has choices when it comes to her care.*

After meeting with their financial professional, Nathan and Emily decide to put a large portion of their savings into an income annuity with a critical care rider. They can trigger the rider benefit when the time comes, so they will have a nice sum of money coming in every month when Emily needs additional care. She can then choose whether she wants to go into a nursing home, or pay someone she is comfortable with to come into their home and help.

TAKING CONTROL OF YOUR FUTURE

Planning for the realities of long term care is about options, choices and independence. Nobody wants to imagine getting sick or moving to an assisted living facility, which is why so often the subject is avoided and left up to chance.

Talking about long term care isn't about planning for a stay in a nursing home. It's about planning for independence. Most people, if given the choice, would prefer the comfort and familiarity of their own home rather than a stay at a facility. Planning ahead for the realities we all face down the road as our bodies age and we get older gives you more options about where you live and with whom, and it protects your spouse or loved ones from the emotional and physical burden.

While Nathan and Emily have very good reasons to plan for long term care costs, most retirees enter into retirement feeling great, and chronic illness is understandably the last thing on their mind. While it's good to plan to be healthy, it's also good to plan for the realities down the road.

Imagine a husband and wife who decided *not* to plan for long term care. The wife maintains her health, but her husband gets sick. After one year of chronic illness, he finds he is no longer able to perform two of the six activities of daily living (known as ADLs,) which include dressing, walking and eating. His wife becomes taxed, both mentally and physically, and so at that point she chooses the easiest option: bringing her husband to a nursing home where he can receive around the clock care. While this is a relief to her at first, the nursing home facility will cost them almost $100,000 annually. How many years can she afford to pay for this before running out money?

There is no need to expose yourself to this risk. It used to be that you either bought an expensive long term care insurance policy or you paid out of pocket. Today's retirees have more options.

Option #1: Traditional Long Term Care Insurance
This is the option most people are familiar with, and it can be a spendy one. You essentially transfer the risk of your long term care expenses onto an insurance company. In exchange for knowing you have contracted protection in place, you pay out an annual premium much like you do with homeowners insurance or car insurance. Long term care insurance becomes more expensive and difficult to get the older you get, because it is your health that qualifies you for this type of insurance. However, the biggest fear most people have regarding this solution is that they will never see the money they paid in. The insurance can only be used to fund long term care costs as set forth by the terms of the contract. If you never need long term care, all the money you have paid into the policy reverts back to the insurance company. Today's retirees have better options.

Option #2 Medicare or Medicaid

Medicare is a federal insurance program paid out of Social Security deductions and available to anyone who has paid into Social Security once certain age or health requirements are met. There are a lot of misconceptions about this option and how it helps senior citizens. Medicare is not designed to cover prolonged stays at nursing homes, but rather funds short-term stays for medical conditions that are expected to improve.* For example, if you qualified for Medicare and were in a nursing home for short term rehabilitation after hip replacement surgery, the program would pay for a maximum of 20 days for skilled care, with an additional 80 days of care that could be purchased with a daily co-payment. If you require a nursing home stay longer than 100 days, then you are on your own when it comes to payment.

Medicaid is a joint federal and state program that can help pay for costs associated with medical and long term care, but there are strict eligibility requirements based on income and asset limits.** Medicaid is considered care for those in need and most people are surprised to find how few assets disqualify them from care. You also have very few choices when it comes to your health care options, because the state controls where you go and who you live with, even if it means your spouse has to drive a far distance in order to visit. Medicaid spend down is a term that refers to legally divesting yourself of your assets in order to qualify for Medicaid's funding of long term care. If you are thinking of qualifying for Medicaid, seek the advice of an elder care law attorney who specializes in Medicaid law.

---

*http://longtermcare.gov/medicare-medicaid-more/medicare/
**http://longtermcare.gov/medicare-medicaid-more/medicaid/

Option #3 Critical Illness Riders

Many of today's life insurance policies and annuity products have riders and provisions for increased income in the event of chronic illness. Even if it's too late to qualify for traditional long term care insurance, long term care riders on annuity and life insurance products might still be an option for you. For example, a fixed indexed annuity with a critical care rider requires no health exam and no underwriting as long as you can perform all six of the ADLs (which include eating, bathing, dressing, toileting, walking and continence.)

This benefit is also known as a home health care doubler, impairment doubler, or an income doubler because the fixed income contracted by the rider will double should you or your spouse require long term care. The inability to perform two out of the 6 ADLs triggers the benefit, which can also include funding of basic custodial services such as cleaning and taking out the garbage, or more involved intrinsic nursing services. With a critical illness rider, the insurance company pays you the money, and you get to control how the money is spent.

Option #4 Life and Long Term Care Combo Plan

More and more people are shying away from the expense of traditional long term care insurance and opting for insurance policies that have both Living Benefits and Death Benefits built right in. Life insurance companies call long term care benefits Living Benefits because you don't have to die in order to receive the money. The plan provides you with the means to pay for home health care or a nursing home facility *while you are alive*, in addition to the death benefit protection of a life insurance policy. This gives both you and your spouse more options and control of your health care.

The cost for these Living Benefits is comparable to the cost of traditional long term care insurance and the policies are funded by monthly payments. Unlike traditional long term care insurance, the money is not lost if there is no need for long term care, because the policy also provides your loved ones with a death benefit. While cost can sometimes be an issue, when you consider the multiple benefits and flexibility offered, many people find these policies preferable.

Option #5 Out of Pocket
Some retirees find themselves unable to qualify for annuity products or long term care insurance. If your medical condition is too far advanced and you are unable to get a solution into place, working with a financial professional to set up an account for this expense can be a viable alternative. With this option, you take a portion of your assets not needed for income generation and set it aside for your long term care needs. When the time comes and either you or your spouse require accelerated health care, you know what funds to tap into.

Planning for the risks that can devastate your retirement will strengthen the foundation of your income plan. When things come up—and they always come up—you will be able to rely on the strength of a well thought-out plan that considers the '*what if*' realities of stock market loss, bereavement and the cost of long term care. While none of these subjects are pleasant to think about, planning for them now will help set you up for more years of enjoyment and success.

» *Even as a toddler, Sam Weston was a careful and considerate kid. As the oldest boy, he shared his toys, washed his hands and thought before jumping off the furniture. As an adult, Sam also thought about his future. He took out a life insurance policy when he and Louise were newly married and just starting their lives. He funded the policy with what he could*

*afford and was told that due to the market earnings, it would
be paid up by the time he was aged 65.*

*Twenty-five years later, Sam is 65 years old, and he and
Louise are ready to retire. The problem is, he has an unexpected monthly expense he didn't plan for. The earnings on the
life insurance policy he took out didn't perform as promised, so
now the monthly premiums have gotten very expensive. Sam
doesn't think he can afford the payments during retirement,
but he still needs the protection. Sam is 65 years old with a
25 year old policy that's not paid up, a monthly premium he
can't afford, and a spouse who may or may not be protected.*

Sam does not have the kind of life insurance that he needs.

DO YOU HAVE THE OLD OR THE NEW LIFE INSURANCE?

Indexed, variable and universal life insurance products all
provide a death benefit to your loved ones should you meet an
early demise. The kind of policy held by Sam in our story above
was an older kind of life insurance known as Variable Universal
Life. There are newer policies available to retirees today that have
market linked earnings combined with additional benefits and
premium guarantees built-in to prevent situations like the one
Sam found himself in. These new policies are known as Indexed
Universal Life insurance, or IULs. Understanding the difference
between the old and the new kind of life insurance can help you
determine whether or not your current policy is what you need as
you get ready to retire.

Variable universal life insurance products have been around
a long time and are sold as a way to invest in the stock market
with your life insurance cash value. Because the investment is tied
directly to market investments such as mutual funds, its value
fluctuates. Investors like Sam purchase a variable policy under the
promise of returns illustrated anywhere between 9 and 12 per-

cent, with a payment premium that underfunds the policy from the start. Sam paid in what he could afford at the time, a reduced annual premium of $50, under the expectation that the market gains would make up for the rest of the funding. What happened, however, was that the cost of the monthly insurance premiums increased as Sam got older and the market did not perform as expected. He was told at the age of 40 that the policy would be paid up at the age of 65, but in reality, his premiums continued to go up and up and now here he is 25 years later, with a policy that is about to lapse because it requires $4,000 in annual funding in order to keep the policy in place.

Today's universal life policies have more benefits and guarantees set in place, including premium guarantees, so you know the annual payments will never go above a set amount. The amount you pay when you purchase the policy is the same amount you will pay throughout the life of the contract regardless of what happens to market rates. Indexed Universal Life is *linked* to market growth without direct market participation, so there are no wild fluctuations. Linked to an index such as the S&P 500, the IUL can benefit from market upsides without the downsides. The interest rate cannot be negative, and you can choose to overfund the policy if that proves to be in your best interest. IULs allow you to grow money tax-deferred, and they also come with additional benefits you can access during your retirement.

Life insurance, like car models, change over time. You have your new models with new upgrades and features, and you have your old models. Some of the things about the old models might be working for you; other things may no longer serve you. It's a good idea to review your life insurance policies periodically to make sure they are still providing you with the protection you need. It can also make sense to review your policies if a specific issue comes up, such as a policy you can no longer afford, or if there is a need for long term care. New life insurance policies with Living Benefits—and these come in the form of term or whole life or indexed universal life—can give you more benefits and options than old policies. As mentioned earlier, a policy with Living Benefits can give you long term care funding and tax-free death benefits paid out to your spouse. A new life insurance policy might make much more sense in a lot of cases if you can qualify.

CLAIMING INDEPENDENCE: WHAT IS A FUNERAL TRUST?

When reviewing your insurance policies, you might find that you have a policy you no longer need. Maybe you bought it to cover your mortgage if you passed away and now the house is paid off. Whatever the reason, if the need for the insurance is no longer there, it might be possible to transfer the funds and use the money for another purpose.

A Funeral Trust is one way you can set aside protected funds to cover your funeral expenses. This is not a type of policy that you have to pay monthly premiums for; instead, you transfer the lump sum cash value from one insurance policy into another. In most cases, a Funeral Trust is same thing as a traditional life insurance policy placed inside of an irrevocable burial trust. This means a Funeral Trust is an asset that you can protect from nursing home spendown. It won't be counted as an asset by Medicaid and the nursing home can't access this money. Instead, the funds can be used to finance any final expenses such as the casket, flowers, or anything related to funeral expenses.

Most retirees don't want to be a burden to their kids, and they want to have the peace of mind that comes from knowing their burial expenses are paid for. Transferring funds to a Funeral Trust is one way you can fund this expense without additional cost to you. Taking control of your assets begins with understanding your assets, the risk they are exposed to, and reviewing policies to make sure they align with your current needs.

CHAPTER 2 RECAP //

- Many people are surprised to find that their current investments aren't aligned with their retirement goals. Multiple retirement accounts can create confusion about risk, tax implications, and safety. Taking control of your assets begins with determining your exposure to risk.

- Assigning colors to money can help you more easily visualize the assets that make up your retirement savings. Green Money is safer and more reliable, Red Money represents assets that are exposed to risk, and Yellow Money is Red Money managed by a professional.

- The Retirement Analyzer is one kind of report your financial professional can run that will help determine the consequences of risk to the health of your retirement income. A holistic plan includes addressing the financial impact of stock market downturns and implementing solutions for spousal continuation and long term care costs.

- Planning for long term care is about maintaining your independence. Today's retirees have more than one solution when it comes to paying for long term care insurance. Traditional insurance can be expensive, but some annuities, when purchased with critical care riders, can provide you with an income doubler to help defray the costs of long-term care.

- Life insurance policies with Living Benefits will pay your beneficiaries when you die as well as paying you while you are still alive to help fund long term care.

- A lot of people are sold investments products under the pretense of unrealistic promises. Some products, such as market-linked universal life insurance, might become underfunded due to an underperforming market. Be sure to have your insurance policies reviewed regularly by a financial professional to make sure they still provide you with the protection that you need.

3

WHAT YOU NEED TO KNOW ABOUT INCOME PLANNING

Will we run out of money during retirement?

During an especially cold June afternoon, Ed Weston suffers a massive heart attack while painting a house and passes away at the age of 60. His wife, Darlene, is devastated. As an only child and never able to have children of her own, Darlene decides that she wants to be around family. Ed left her with some nice investments and the proceeds from a life insurance policy. She uses this money to travel to Wausau, Wisconsin, so she can be near Ed's family.

Darlene spends an entire summer in a rented cabin along the Wisconsin river, visiting with George and Dee and Ed's older brothers and their families. She uses her money to pay for her rental cabin while maintaining her bills and taking time off from her job in

Chicago. She also showers her nieces and nephews with presents and trips to water parks, go-cart racing and roller coaster rides. Then she decides to take everybody to Disneyland.

This buying spree seems to help her during her time of grief, but when Darlene gets home, she faces a terrifying awakening. Darlene is just a few years away from retiring, and yet she has just blown 40 percent of the money she would be relying on for income.

How will she support herself during retirement?

The most essential element to retirement planning is the ability of your savings to provide you with the income you need. Your assets should be viewed as the resource for creating this income to be enjoyed either now or a few years down the road. For some people, this will be an obvious reality, but for others, this transition will be more difficult. As a society, we tend to be paycheck cashers: we spend the money we have on what we need now, without a whole lot of concern for later. While Darlene certainly needed to spend time with family during her grieving process, the mistake she made was not securing her income *needs* first before indulging her income *wants*.

Proper income planning begins with an understanding of your monthly obligations. Once you know what that number is, you can then focus on supplemental income. If Darlene had met with her financial professional prior to spending down her assets, she could have been better directed. Prior to her spending spree, Darlene had ample funds to secure her retirement. She could have put a plan in place that allowed a generous income allowance *and* a discretionary fund for trips and time with family. Had Darlene secured her income first, she would have been able to retire at an early age comfortably and without worry.

Make the time to put a plan in place. Take a moment to evaluate your daily income needs. Finding the most efficient and beneficial way to address your monthly obligations directly impacts your lifestyle and improves your ability to do more of the things you want to do like travel and spending time with the family. Let's revisit your income goals:

- What is your lifestyle today?
- Would you like to maintain it into retirement?
- Are you meeting your needs?
- Are you happy with your lifestyle?
- What do you really *need* to live on when you retire?

Some people will have the luxury of maintaining or improving their lifestyle, while others may have to make decisions about what they need versus what they want during their retirement. Once you have identified your income need, you will know what percentage of Green Money investments to structure for income and how much to set aside for accumulation needs down the road.

WHAT'S REALISTIC? HOW MUCH MONEY DO YOU NEED

Every financial strategy for retirement needs first to accommodate the day-to-day need for income. Most people don't have a clear number when it comes to their monthly financial obligations, and are surprised to find that during retirement, expenses can actually rise. Once they are no longer working, retirees find themselves enjoying their free time. They want to go out to dinner, travel and have adventures. All of this costs money. Ask yourself, what day of the week do you spend the most money? For most people, the answer is Saturday, or a day they are not working. Retirement is one long series of work-free days, so ask yourself, what will you be doing?

To answer the question—how much money do I need?—start with a household budget. Your financial professional can take you through a budgeting process that lists every possible expense so you can arrive at a realistic number. Most people are surprised to find that the final number is higher than they thought.

How Much Money Do You Need? While this amount will be different for everyone, the general rule of thumb is that a retiree will require 70 to 80 percent of their pre-retirement income to maintain their lifestyle. Once you know what that number is, the key becomes matching your income need with the correct investment strategies, options and tools to satisfy that need.

WHEN DO YOU NEED YOUR INCOME?

The moment your working income ceases and you start living off the money you've set aside for retirement is referred to as the **retirement cliff**. When you begin drawing income from your retirement assets, you have entered the distribution phase of your financial plan. ***The distribution phase of your retirement plan*** is when you reach the point of relying on your assets for income. This is where your Green Money comes into play: the safer, more reliable assets that you have accumulated that are designed to provide you with a steady income.

On day one of your retirement, you will need a steady and reliable supply of income from your Green Money. There are new indexed annuity products currently available that are designed to address the longevity concerns of today's retirees. These products provide protection of principal with growth and a guaranteed income stream for life, no matter how long you live. We will talk about how to use investment products for income creation in Chapter Four: Filling the Income Gap.

How long does your income need to last? Are there certain expenses you expect to crop up in the future such as health care costs? Are you expecting to inherit some money? Do you plan to liquidate assets such as a home or real estate? When you take health care costs, potential emergencies, plans for moving or traveling, and other retirement expenses into account, you can really give your calculator a workout. While you want to reduce the amount of Red Money you have and to transition it to Green Money, you don't necessarily need all of it to generate income for you right away. You want to maximize retirement benefits to meet *your lifetime income needs.*

WHO DO YOU NEED IT FOR?

Poverty after the loss of a spouse is more common among women than men.* Many women find they have fewer options of guaranteed income sources or, like Darlene, they make money decisions during times of grief without planning first. Avoiding poverty as a retired widow means making a plan now, so when and if the hard times come, you're prepared and have a solid plan to follow.

What would your retirement income look like if one spouse passed away? If your husband or wife is receiving a traditional pension, will that income source disappear when they die? What will your Social Security benefit look like if you were to receive only one check instead of two? There are many investment tools designed to provide spousal continuation, such as life insurance policies that provide for tax-free income and newer indexed products that offer a joint life option so both spouses are protected against income loss. Still other couples choose to set aside a separate account with an income rider that is allowed to grow and isn't turned on until the money is needed.

Regardless of what option you choose, it's important for both spouses to be involved in the income planning process. If your husband or wife handles all the accounts, make sure you understand how much income will be coming if he or she passes away. Also find out whether or not that income comes from a guaranteed source.

*http://www.ssa.gov/policy/docs/ssb/v65n3/v65n3p31.html

READ
Y, SET, RETIRE!

WHERE IS THIS MONEY COMING FROM?

The first place we look for income producing sources are Safe Money options such as pensions and Social Security. The amount of income provided by those sources can't be changed, and they provide the retirement base that you build up from until you reach the number you need. A financial professional can help you customize a solid income plan based on your retirement goals and future needs.

CHAPTER 3 RECAP //

- The foundation of a retirement strategy depends on knowing how much money you need, when you need it and who you need it to provide for.
- Spousal continuation is one area often overlooked by retirees. When one spouse dies, the loss of pensions and monetary benefits such as Social Security means a reduction in monthly income. Your income plan should take into consideration guaranteed sources of income that will still be available after your spouse passes away.
- Some annuities offer joint life options with the purchase of an income rider. These income riders continue to supply a monthly income even after one spouse passes away as opposed to single income riders.

52

4

HOW TO GET THE MOST OUT OF SOCIAL SECURITY

Does it matter when I take my Social Security benefit?

Sam is the oldest child of George and Dee Weston. He stayed in Marathon County and worked 30 years at the hardware manufacturing plant while his wife, Louise, stayed home with their kids, Jack and Maggie. Later when the kids got older, Louise got a part-time job at the grocery store.

As they look at their options for retirement income, Louise realizes that her Social Security benefit is much lower than her husband's— only $1,500 a month—while Sam is entitled to $3,000 a month if he lets the money "roll up" and waits until he is 70 before claiming his benefit. Louise wants to retire now and start spending more time with *the grandkids, but how can they do this if Sam has to wait until he is 70 before receiving a benefit check?*

Louise attends a Social Security workshop to learn more about something called Spousal Benefits. She makes an appointment with a financial professional who can run a Social Security Optimization Report and is delighted to learn that Sam can file a Restricted Application. This will give him a benefit check of 50 percent of what she is entitled to if he files when he turns 66, at Full Retirement Age. He can still allow his benefit to grow and roll up, so at the age of 70 he will claim his full $3,000 a month, but in the meantime, he is eligible to receive an additional $750 a month. This $750 a month allows the couple to meet their income goals.

There are a lot of terms and phrases associated with Social Security benefits such as FRAs, PIAs and "roll up." There are also hundreds of different options and choices that a married couple can make when filing for their Social Security benefit. Louise and Sam utilized a Restricted Application option, but there are many other combinations possible for a married couple filing for the Social Security benefits:

- You both file for benefits.
- You suspend benefits and your spouse files.
- Spouse suspends and you file.
- You file a restricted application and your spouse files.
- Spouse files restricted and you file.
- You suspend and spouse files restricted.
- Spouse suspends and you file restricted.

There are also additional benefits married people are entitled to in the event of divorce or death. Educating yourself about these options and terms can help you get the most out of this important monthly benefit.

COLLECT SOME NOW AND MORE LATER

The Retired Worker Benefit is what most people are talking about when they refer to Social Security. This is your benefit based on your earnings and the amount that you have paid into the system over the span of your career. There are five other benefits that most people aren't as familiar with that are especially important for married couples. Learning how these benefits can maximize your lifetime income just might give you a way to collect some money *now* while allowing your benefit to grow, or roll-up, so you can collect *even more money later.*

File and Suspend: This concept allows you to file at age 66 (which is Full Retirement Age or FRA) and suspend the benefit. This means your benefit amount will continue to roll up, or grow each year at a rate of 8 percent. Once you file and suspend, you can trigger the benefit any time you want, but after age 70, the benefit no longer grows. Waiting to claim your benefit allows you to receive a higher lifetime benefit, but if you have health concerns, this might not be a good option for you.

Restricted Application: This is the benefit that Sam and Louise utilized in our story example above. A higher-earning spouse may be able to start collecting a portion of the lower-earning spousal benefit while allowing his or her benefit to continue to grow. Be clear when you file that you are restricting the application to the spousal benefit only, and not collecting your own benefit. This strategy can help maximize your overall lifetime family benefit.

Spousal Benefit: The Spousal Benefit is a good option when one spouse's benefit is significantly lower than the others. This benefit can work in tandem with File and Suspend. The lower-earning spouse is eligible to receive up to 50 percent of the higher-earning spouse's benefit without triggering their own benefit. For example, if your wife is eligible to receive $2,000 a month, and your benefit is only $500 a month, you can File and Suspend and then claim the Spousal Benefit. Your own benefit continues to grow at the 8 percent rate. At the same time, you will receive 50 percent of your spouse's benefit, which in this case amounts to an extra check for $1,000 a month.

Divorced Spouse: If you have gone through a divorce and were married for at least 10 years, you might be eligible to receive 50 percent of your former spouse's benefit. There are a few qualifications that must be met before you can receive this benefit:
- You were married to your former spouse for at least 10 years.
- You are at least 62 years old.
- You are currently single and thus not eligible for the Spousal Benefits mentioned above.
- You aren't entitled to a higher Social Security benefit on your own record.*

Survivor Benefit: This benefit allows the surviving spouse to receive the higher of the two benefits in the event of death. For example, if your wife is eligible to receive $3,000 a month and your benefit is only $1,000 a month, your income would drop significantly should your wife pass away. The Survivor Benefit dictates that in the event of her death, you could elect the higher of the two benefits. Instead of only receiving $1,000 a month, you would receive $3,000. Many widows don't know about this benefit and are living near or in poverty due to lack of knowledge.

---

*SSA.gov/retire2/yourdivspouse.htm

WHERE SHOULD YOU GO TO FOR ADVICE?

Social Security is a guaranteed, Green Money source of income that is an important part of the big picture when it comes to the longevity of your income during retirement. Social Security employees can give you information, but they are banned from providing advice and recommendations about how you can maximize your individual situation. If you want a truly accurate understanding of when and how to file, you need someone who will ask you the right questions about your situation, someone who has access to specialized software that can crunch the numbers. The reality is that you need to work with a professional that can provide you with the sophisticated analysis of your situation that will help you make a truly informed decision.

Ideally, you want to work with a financial professional who can run a Social Security Optimization Report. The Social Security Optimization Report is not a product we sell but a service that we offer. The report generates an individualized understanding of how and when to file for your Social Security to get the most out of this important benefit. When you get your customized Social Security Maximization Report, you will not only know all of the options available to you—but you will understand the financial implications of each choice. In addition to the analysis, you will also get a report that shows *exactly* at what age—including which month and year—you should trigger benefits and how you should apply. It also includes a variety of other time-specific recommendations, such as when to apply for Medicare or take Required Minimum Distributions from your qualified plans. A report means there is no need to wonder, or to try to figure out when to take action—the Social Security Maximization Report lays it all out for you in plain English.

SOCIAL SECURITY 101: THE BASICS

Here are some facts that illustrate how Americans currently use
Social Security:

- 90 percent of Americans age 65 and older receive Social
  Security benefits.*
- Social Security provides 39 percent of income for retired
  Americans.*
- Claiming Social Security benefits at the wrong time can
  reduce your monthly benefit by up to 57 percent.**
- 43 percent of men and 48 percent of women claim Social
  Security benefits at age 62. **
- 74 percent of retirees receive reduced Social Security
  benefits.**
- In 2013, the average monthly Social Security benefit was
  $1,261. *The maximum benefit for 2013 was $2,533. The
  $1,272 monthly benefit reduction between the average and
  the maximum is applied for life.* ***

There are many aspects of Social Security that are well known
and others that aren't. Social Security is a massive government
program that manages retirement benefits for millions of people.
Experts spend their entire careers understanding and analyzing it.
Luckily, you don't have to understand all of the intricacies of Social Security to maximize its advantages. You simply need to know
the best way to manage your Social Security benefit. You need to
know exactly what to do to get the most from your Social Security
benefit and when to do it. Taking the time to create a roadmap for
your Social Security strategy will help ensure that you are able to

---

*http://www.ssa.gov/pressoffice/basicfact.htm
**When to Claim Social Security Benefits, David Blanchett, CFA, CFP® January,
2013
***http://www.socialsecurity.gov/pressoffice/factsheets/colafacts2013.com

exact your maximum benefit and efficiently coordinate it with the rest of your retirement plan.

There are many aspects of Social Security that you have no control over. You don't control how much you put into it, and you don't control what it's invested in or how the government manages it. **However, you do control when and how you file for benefits.** The real question about Social Security that you need to answer is, "When should I start taking Social Security?" While this is the all-important question, there are a couple of key pieces of information you need to track down first. Before we get into the calculations and strategies, let's start by covering the basic information about Social Security which should give you an idea of where you stand.

Eligibility. Understanding how and when you are eligible for Social Security benefits will help clarify what to expect when the time comes to claim them.

To receive retirement benefits from Social Security, you must earn eligibility. In almost all cases, Americans born after 1929 must earn 40 quarters of credit to be eligible to draw their Social Security retirement benefit. In 2013, a Social Security credit represents $1,160 earned in a calendar quarter. The number changes as it is indexed each year, but not drastically. In 2012, a credit represented $1,130. Four quarters of credit is the maximum number that can be earned each year. In 2013, an American would have had to earn at least $4,640 to accumulate four credits. In order to qualify for retirement benefits, you must have earned a minimum number of credits. Additionally, if you are at least 62 years old and have been married to a recipient of Social Security benefits for at least 12 months, you can choose to receive Spousal Benefits. Although 40 is the minimum number of credits required to begin drawing benefits, it is important to know that once you claim your Social Security benefit, there is no going back. Although there may be cost of living adjustments made, you are locked into that base benefit amount forever.

Primary Insurance Amount. You can think of your Primary Insurance Amount (PIA) like a ripening fruit. It represents the amount of your Social Security benefit at your Full Retirement Age (FRA). Your benefit becomes fully ripe at your FRA, and will neither reduce nor increase due to early or delayed retirement options. If you opt to take benefits before your FRA, however, your monthly benefit will be less than your PIA. You will essentially be picking an unripened fruit. On the one hand, waiting until after your FRA to access your benefits will increase your benefit beyond your PIA. On the other hand, you don't want the fruit to overripen, because every month you wait is one less check you get from the government.

Full Retirement Age. Your FRA is an important figure for anyone who is planning to rely on Social Security benefits in their retirement. Depending on when you were born, there is a specific age at which you will attain FRA. Your FRA is dictated by your year of birth and is the age at which you can begin your full monthly benefit. Your FRA is important because it is half of the equation used to calculate your Social Security benefit. The other half of the equation is based on when you start taking benefits.

When Social Security was initially set up, the FRA was age 65, and it still is for people born before 1938. But as time has passed, the age for receiving full retirement benefits has increased. If you were born between 1938 and 1960, your full retirement age is somewhere on a sliding scale between 65 and 67. Anyone born in 1960 or later will now have to wait until age 67 for full benefits. Increasing the FRA has helped the government reduce the cost of the Social Security program, which pays out more than a half trillion dollars to beneficiaries every year!*

While you can begin collecting benefits as early as age 62, the amount you receive as a monthly benefit will be less than it would be if you wait until you reached your FRA or surpass your FRA. It is important to note that if you file for Social Security benefit before your FRA, *the reduction to your monthly benefit will remain in place for the rest of your life.* You can also delay receiving benefits up to age 70, in which case your benefits will be higher than your PIA for the rest of your life.

- At FRA, 100 percent of PIA is available as a monthly benefit.
- At age 62, your Social Security retirement benefits are available. For each month you take benefits prior to your FRA, however, the monthly amount of your benefit is reduced. *This reduction stays in place for the rest of your life.*
- At age 70, your monthly benefit reaches its maximum. After you turn age 70, your monthly benefit will no longer increase.

Year of Birth	Full Retirement Age
1943-1954	66
1955	66 and 2 months
1956	66 and 4 months
1957	66 and 6 months
1958	66 and 8 months
1959	66 and 10 months
1960 or later	age 67**

*http://www.ssa.gov/pressoffice/basicfact.htm
**http://www.ssa.gov/OACT/progdata/nra.html

ROLLING UP YOUR SOCIAL SECURITY

Your Social Security income "rolls up" the longer you wait to claim it. Your monthly benefit will continue to increase until you turn 70 years old. But because Social Security is the foundation of most people's retirement, many Americans feel that they don't have control over how or when they receive their benefits. As a matter of fact, only 4 percent of Americans wait until after their FRA to file for benefits! This trend persists, despite the fact that every dollar you increase your Social Security income by means less money you will have to spend from your nest egg to meet your retirement income needs! For many people, creating their Social Security strategy is the most important decision they can make to positively impact their retirement. ***The difference between the best and worst Social Security decision can be tens of thousands of dollars over a lifetime of benefits—up to $170,000!***

Deciding NOW or LATER: Following the above logic, it makes sense to wait as long as you can to begin receiving your Social Security benefit. However, the answer isn't always that simple. Not everyone has the option of waiting. Many people need to rely on Social Security on day one of their retirement. In fact, ***nearly 50 percent of 62-year-old Americans file for Social Security benefits.*** Why is this number so high? Some might need the income. Others might be in poor health and don't feel they will live long enough to make FRA worthwhile for themselves or their families. It is also possible, however, that the majority of folks taking an early benefit at age 62 are simply under-informed about Social Security. Perhaps they make this major decision based on rumors and emotion.

File Immediately if You:
- Find your job is unbearable.
- Are willing to sacrifice retirement income.
- Are not healthy and need a reliable source of income.

Consider Delaying Your Benefit if You:
- Want to maximize your retirement income.
- Want to increase retirement benefits for your spouse.
- Are still working and like it.
- Are healthy and willing / able to wait to file.

So if you decide to wait, how long should you wait? Lots of people can put it off for a few years, but not everyone can wait until they are 70 years old. Your individual circumstances may be able to help you determine when you should begin taking Social Security. If you do the math, you will quickly see that between ages 62 and 70, there are 96 months in which you can file for your Social Security benefit. If you take into account those 96 months and the 96 months your spouse could also file for Social Security, along with the number of different strategies for structuring your benefit, you can easily end up with more than 20,000 different scenarios. It's safe to say this isn't the kind of math that most people can easily handle. Each month would result in a different benefit amount. The longer you wait, the higher your monthly benefit amount becomes. Each month you wait, however, is one less month that you receive a Social Security check.

The goal is to maximize your lifetime benefits. That may not always mean waiting until you can get the largest monthly payment. Taking the bigger picture into account, you want to find out how to get the most money out of Social Security over the number of years that you draw from it. Don't underestimate the power of optimizing your benefit: the difference between the BEST and WORST Social Security election can easily be between $30,000 to $50,000 in lifetime benefits. *The difference can be very substantial!*

If you know that every month you wait, your Social Security benefit goes up a little bit, and you also know that every month you wait, you receive one less benefit check, how do you determine where the sweet spot is that maximizes your benefits over your lifetime? Financial professionals have access to software that will calculate the best year and month for you to file for benefits based on your default life expectancy. You can further customize that information by estimating your life expectancy based on your health, habits and family history. If you can then create an income plan (we'll get into this later in the chapter) that helps you wait until the target date for you to file for Social Security, you can optimize your retirement income strategy to get the most out of your Social Security benefit. How can you calculate your life expectancy? Well, you don't know exactly how long you'll live, but you have a better idea than the government does. They rely on averages to make their calculations. *You have much more personal information about your health, lifestyle and family history than they do.* You can use that knowledge to game the system and beat all the other people who are making uninformed decisions by filing early for Social Security.

While you can and should educate yourself about how Social Security works, the reality is you don't need to know a lot of general information about Social Security in order to make choices about your retirement. What you do need to know is exactly *what to do to maximize your benefit.* Because knowing what you need to do has huge impacts on your retirement! For most Americans, Social Security is the foundation of income planning for retirement. Social Security benefits represent nearly 40 percent of the income of retirees.* For many people, it can represent the largest portion of their retirement income. Not treating your Social Security benefit as an asset and investment tool can lead to sub-optimization of your largest source of retirement income.

Let's take a look at an example that shows the impact of working with a financial professional to optimize Social Security benefits:

---

*http://www.socialsecurity.gov/pressoffice/basicfact.htm

» *Nathan and Emily Weston are a typical American couple who have worked their whole lives and saved when they could. Emily was diagnosed with MS in her thirties, but with newer drugs and better care, her prognosis was good and her life expectancy about average. They began meeting with their financial professional years ago, in order to address legacy concerns and plan for their long term care needs. Now that they are both older—Nathan was 60 years old and Emily was 56 years old—they wanted to learn about how to maximize their Social Security. They sat down with their financial professional who logged onto the Social Security website to look up their PIAs. Nathan's PIA was $1,900 and Emily's was $900.*

If the Westons cash in at age 62 and begin taking retirement benefits from Social Security, they would receive an estimated $492,000 in lifetime benefits. That may seem like a lot, but if you divide that amount over 20 years, it averages out to be just shy of $25,000 per year. The Westons were accustomed to a more significant annual income than that. To make up the difference, they would have to rely on alternative retirement income options. They will basically have to depend on a bigger nest egg to provide them with the income they need.

If they wait until their FRA, they will increase their lifetime benefits to an estimated $523,700. This option allows them to achieve their Primary Insurance Amount, which will provide them a $33,000 annual income.

After learning the Westons' needs and using software to calculate the most optimal time to begin drawing benefits, the Westons' financial professional determined that the best option for them drastically increases their potential lifetime benefits to $660,000!

*By using strategies that their financial professional recom-
mended, they increased their potential lifetime benefits by as
much as $148,000. There's no telling how much you could
miss out on from your Social Security if you don't take time to
create a strategy that calculates your maximum benefit. For
the Westons, the value of maximizing their benefits was the
difference between night and day. While this may seem like a
special case, it isn't uncommon to find benefit increases of this
magnitude. You'll never know unless you take a look at your
own options.*

Despite the importance of knowing when and how to take your
Social Security benefit, many of today's retirees and pre-retirees
may know little about the mechanics of Social Security and how
they can maximize their benefit.

MAXIMIZING YOUR LIFETIME BENEFIT

As discussed in Chapter 2, calculating how to maximize **lifetime
benefits** is more important than waiting until age 70 for your
maximum **monthly benefit amount.** It's about getting the most
income during your lifetime. Professional benefit maximization
software can target the year and month that it is most beneficial
for you to file based on your life expectancy.

The three most common ages that people associate with retirement benefits are 62 (Earliest Eligible Age), 66 (Full Retirement
Age), and 70 (age at which monthly maximum benefit is reached).
In almost all circumstances, however, none of those three most
common ages will give you the maximum lifetime benefit.

Remember, every month you wait to file, the amount of your
benefit check goes up, but you also get one less check. With all of
the different options, strategies and benefits to choose from, you
can see why filing for Social Security is more complicated than
just mailing in the paperwork. Gathering the data and making

yourself aware of all your different options isn't enough to know exactly what to do, however. On the one hand, you can knock yourself out trying to figure out which options are best for you and wondering if you made the best decision. On the other hand, you can work with a financial professional who uses customized software that takes all the variables of your specific situation into account and calculates your best option.

You have tens of thousands of different options for filing for your Social Security benefit. You don't know exactly how long you're going to live, but you have a better idea of your life expectancy than the actuaries at the Social Security Administration who can only work with averages. They can't make calculations based on your specific situation. A professional can run the numbers for you and get the target date that maximizes your potential lifetime benefits. You can't get this information from the SSA, but you *can* get it from a financial professional.

Review Questions about Your Social Security Benefit:
- How can I maximize my lifetime benefit? By knowing when and how to file for Social Security. This usually means waiting until you have at least reached your Full Retirement Age. A professional has the experience and the tools to help determine when and how you can maximize your lifetime benefits.
- Who will provide reliable advice for making these decisions? Only a professional has the tools and experience to provide you reliable advice.
- Will the Social Security Administration provide me with the advice? The Social Security Administration cannot provide you with advice or strategies for claiming your benefit. They can give you information about your monthly benefit, but that's it. They also don't have the tools to tell you what your specific best option is. They can accurately answer how the

system works, but they can't advise you on what decision to make as to how and when to file for benefits

CHAPTER 4 RECAP //

- You cannot get advice about how to maximize your lifetime benefit from a Social Security representative. They are prohibited from giving advice about when to elect your benefit options.
- There are several important benefits for married couples that can provide additional income. These benefits include the following: Restricted Application, File and Suspend, Spousal Benefit, Divorced Spouse benefit, and the Survivor Benefit.
- To get the most out of your Social Security benefit, you need to file at the right time. Every dollar your Social Security income increases is less money you'll have to spend from your retirement savings to supplement your income.
- An Investment Advisor can help you determine when you should file for Social Security to get your Maximum Lifetime Benefit.
- Deciding when to take your Social Security benefit is one of the most important decisions you make as a retiree. After the first year of taking the benefit, that amount is locked in for the duration of your lifetime.
- Social Security is a massive, government-funded program and there are many things about this program that you cannot control. You can, however, control when and how you file for benefits.

5

FILLING THE INCOME GAP
WHAT IF SOCIAL SECURITY ISN'T ENOUGH?

Is this investment too good to be true?

Charles and Lucy Weston are now 62 years old and have decided to run the numbers to see what their retirement is going to look like. They know they currently need $6,000 per month to pay their bills and maintain their current lifestyle. They have also done their Social Security homework and have determined that, between the two of them, they will receive $4,200 per month in benefits. They also receive $350 per month in rent from a tenant who lives in a small carriage house in their backyard. Between their Social Security and the monthly rent income, they will be short $1,450 per month.

They do have an additional asset, however. They have been contributing for years to an IRA that has reached a value of $350,000.

They realize that they have to figure out how to turn the $350,000 in their IRA into $1,450 per month for the rest of their life.

At first glance, it may seem like they will have plenty of money. With some quick calculations, they find they have 240 months, or nearly 20 years, of monthly income before they exhaust the account. When you consider income tax, the potential for higher taxes in the future, and market fluctuations (because many IRAs are invested in the market), the amount in the IRA seems to have a little less clout. Every dollar Charles and Lucy take out of the IRA is subject to income tax, and if they leave the remainder in the IRA, they run the risk of losing money in a volatile market. Once they retire and stop getting a paycheck every two weeks, they also stop contributing to their IRA. And when they aren't supplementing its growth with their own money, they are entirely dependent on market growth. That's a scary prospect. They could also withdraw the money from the IRA and put it in a savings account or CD, but removing all the money at once will put them in a tax bracket that will claim a huge portion of the value of the IRA. A seemingly straightforward asset has now become a complicated equation. Charles and Lucy don't know what to do.

After assessing your income needs and maximizing your Social Security, you will then calculate the difference between the guaranteed sources of income you have and the income you need. If your monthly Social Security check and your other supplemental income leave a shortfall, this is called the **Income Gap.** It needs to be filled in order to maintain your lifestyle into retirement, and ideally you want to know how to fill that income gap with the fewest dollars possible.

This is where your retirement savings comes into play. Like Charles and Lucy you may have a pension, an IRA or Roth IRA, dividends from stock holdings, money from the sale of real estate, rental property, or other sources of income. But how can these assets be structured so as to provide a protected, guaranteed source of income you can't outlive? Ideally, you want an investment tool that can guarantee your principal, provide growth that keeps up with inflation, and an income stream you can count on. Is there a way to achieve this ideal in today's less-than-ideal economy?

TAKING A COMPREHENSIVE APPROACH TO YOUR INCOME NEEDS

You looked at Social Security strategies earlier, discovering you have some control over how and when you file. Those decisions can change the outcome of your benefit in your favor. Once you start drawing that income, it will provide you with a reliable source of income for the rest of your life. While there are many factors of Social Security that you can control, there are many that you cannot.

For example, you do not have the choice of putting more money into Social Security in order to get more out of it. If you could have the option to contribute more money toward Social Security in order to secure a guaranteed income, it would be a great way to create a Green Money asset that would enhance your retirement. Since that option isn't available, you may seek an investment tool that is similar to Social Security that provides you with a reliable income. It also has the potential to increase the value of your principal investment! This kind of win-win situation exists, and it's called an annuity.

Today, you probably have savings in a variety of assets that you acquired over the years. But you may not have taken time to examine them and assess how they will support your retirement.

It's not about whether the market goes up or down, but when it does. If it goes down at the wrong time for your five or 10 year retirement horizon, you could be in serious danger of losing some of your retirement income.

If you have assets that you would like to structure for retirement income, ***an annuity may be the right choice for you.***

Ask yourself the following questions:
- How concerned are you about finding a secure financial vehicle to protect your savings?
- How concerned are you that there may be a better way to structure your savings?

If you are concerned about the best way to fill your income gap, an income annuity investment tool is likely a good option for you. Income annuities have many similar qualities to Social Security that give them the same look and feel as that reliable benefit check you get every month. Most importantly, an income annuity such as a Fixed Indexed Annuity (FIA) can be an efficient and profitable way to solve your income gap.

WHAT YOU THINK YOU KNOW ABOUT ANNUITIES

Of all the investment tools out there, annuities have garnered an interesting and largely unfavorable reputation. It's really not the fault of the annuity, but neither is it the fault of the investor. Comparing annuities is like comparing apples to oranges, with one type in particular so different from the others, it can sour the lot like rotten fruit in the barrel. Another factor adding to the confusion is that annuities have changed over the years. The benefits that today's annuities offer retirees are very different from the benefits offered 30 years ago, which is another reason so many people have misperceptions.

Before launching into an education about what today's newer annuities can do for you, let's take a few minutes to cover the list most people have for not liking annuities at all. We'll address these common misperceptions one by one, and provide you with answers about what today's annuities can do for you in terms of income generation and guarantees.

#1: All Annuities have high fees.

If you have heard rotten things about annuities and high fees, a variable annuity is likely the culprit. In Chapter Two, Taking Control of Your Assets, Nathan and Emily had two variable annuities that were costing them an exorbitant amount in fees. Variable annuities are a Red Money investment linked to the stock market and the principal balance of a variable annuity is not guaranteed. More to the point, the fees on these annuities can significantly impact your net returns. In addition to income rider fees, variable annuities are connected to multiple mutual funds with a fee attached for the management of each fund. These fees are in addition to the Mortality and Expense fees (listed as M&E fees) and administrative fees. If you add these fees to an income rider or death benefit, the fees on a variable annuity can exceed 4 percent per year.

#2: If I put my money into an annuity, I'll never get all of it back.

This misperception is based on the function of one kind of annuity still available today called *an immediate annuity* with a lifetime income option. If you put your money in an immediate annuity, then it means what its name suggests: the investment starts paying you an income immediately and the principal is said to be *annuitized.* In exchange for this immediate and guaranteed income, you give up access to your principal.

Today's fixed indexed annuities not only offer some liquidity, they also offer you the ability to create a lifelong income stream while still maintaining control of your principal. You achieve this by purchasing an add-on feature known as an income rider. Some Fixed Indexed Annuities (FIAs) also offer a Minimum Guaranteed Cash Value, also known as a MGCV, which assures you that you will get at least your entire contributed premiums back plus interest when the annuity has matured.

In general, the longer you can set your annuity for growth, the more generous your rate of return will be and the more likely you are to see penalties for early surrender. You have control over what you decide. Annuities that come with the longest terms of surrender and the highest penalties typically pay the highest rate of interest to your annuity. Shorter terms with smaller penalties exist, and they pay lower rates. In either case, **once an annuity is mature, you can take the lump sum and move it, or do anything else with it you like without any penalty.** You can also renew it and keep it going. With an annuity that hasn't been renewed, there will never be any more early withdrawal charges because it is past the surrender charge period.

#3: If I put my money in an annuity and take an income stream, and something happens to me, the insurance company will keep all the proceeds.

The annuities of yesterday worked very much like a pension in that once the investor passed away, the money reverted back to the insurance company. While today's pensions still operate this way, today's newer annuities don't. Fixed and indexed annuities offer many attractive benefits to your beneficiaries and loved ones. With a joint income rider, you can be sure that your spouse will continue to receive the income stream even after you pass away. Any money left in the account value at the time of your death reverts back to your designated beneficiaries.

New FIAs with income riders give you tremendous flexibility when it comes to starting or stopping an income stream, and any money that you don't use goes to your beneficiaries. Income riders do come with a fee—usually around 1 percent—but in exchange for this fee, you have the ability to create both a lifetime income stream and a legacy without giving up access to your principal.

ANNUITIES: YESTERDAY VS TODAY

Annuities have been around since Roman times as an investment tool designed for the purpose of income creation. They have the ability to provide both income and guarantees, but there are annuities out there that are Red Money investments and annuities that can link to market gains without market risk. The following annuity primer is designed to help educate you about which annuities are best suited for your specific income needs.

OLD ANNUITIES:

Single Premium Immediate Annuities (SPIAs)

A Single Premium Immediate Annuity is simply a contract between you and an insurance company that allows you to convert a lump sum of money into an income you can start drawing on next month for an agreed-upon time period. That time period could be five years, or it could be for the remainder of your lifetime. In exchange for this lifetime income stream, you give up control of your principal. With an SPIA, you do not have access to the lump sum of your investment. You give up this access in order to receive the guaranteed income stream.

Oftentimes, people make the mistake of simply choosing the highest lifetime benefit when purchasing an SPIA, but this option may not provide you with the guarantees that you need to protect your spouse or beneficiaries. Make sure to ask your financial professional about your options for putting a guarantee on the contract. Guarantees from insurance companies are based on the claims-paying ability of the issuing insurance company.

Another downside to an SPIA is that you are locked into whatever the interest rate is at the time you purchase the contract. While this interest rate is guaranteed to never drop, it will never go up, either. If today's interest rate gives you enough opportunity to meet your income needs, and you do not need access to the principal, then a SPIA is one way to reduce your risk while giving you regular payments that begin right after you buy the contract.

Variable Annuities
This type of annuity is a securities product and as such, you can only purchase them from a licensed securities agent. They may and often do have a place in retirement planning; however, there are other safer, Green Money alternatives. With a variable annuity, you assume the investment risk. In annuities offered by life insurance companies (such as the FIA,) you don't. When you purchase a variable annuity, the company offers the investor a choice of mutual funds, and the value of these funds will fluctuate with the market. As such, variable annuities are considered Red Money investments.

A lot of people are sold variable annuities without understanding their fee structure or how they work. Unlike FIAs, these annuities do not take advantage of annual reset when the market goes down. The income rider will stay the same, but the value of your actual contract may fall. If you surrender the annuity, the insurance company will pay you the market value of the asset, regardless of whether it matches, exceeds or falls short of the value at which you bought the contract. If its value has dropped significantly, you may be better off taking the income rider without surrendering your contract.

Another drawback of variable annuities is their fee structure. They have administrative costs, mortality and expense costs, surrender charges, and the net expense ratios for the investments of the account. When you total these up, they can be very expensive.

Fixed Annuities
Unlike variable rate annuities, fixed rate annuities have values that do not fluctuate with the stock market and the insurance companies are contractually obligated to pay the fixed rate. These

annuities are contracts with insurance companies and as such they have contractual guarantees within them. Fixed annuities are similar to the way a bank CD functions in that when you purchase the investment, the interest rate and duration is clearly stated, but fixed annuities usually offer more generous returns. You can choose a bank CD earning 1.7 percent for a 5 year period, or a fixed annuity earning 3 percent for that same 5 year period. The money in a fixed annuity also grows tax-deferred, which means you don't owe taxes on the gains until you pull the money out.

The downside of fixed annuities is that the interest rate is locked in. As such, you may miss out on an opportunity for higher growth during the time commitment when your annuity is locked into a fixed rate.

NEW ANNUITIES:

Today's newest annuity is the Fixed Indexed Annuity, also known as the FIA and formerly known as the Equity Indexed annuity, or EIA. Before we launch into a discussion about this versatile investment tool, it bears mentioning that **newer fixed annuities** also exist. Newer fixed annuities such as the Multi-Year Guarantee Annuity (MYGA) can have a place in your overall income plan, especially if you have an income gap for a specific period of time that needs to be filled.

Fixed Indexed Annuities

FIAs are a specialized type of annuity created in the middle to late '90s, known for their ability to generate earnings that are pretty substantial. The key to how well these annuities perform is a feature known as Annual Reset. Annual Reset means that your gains for the year are locked in and added to the base amount of your principal. These gains aren't exposed to loss, which is pretty good when you consider their average rate of return. The worst you can do with an FIA is to make a zero gain. You can never go backwards. Unlike a variable annuity that can fluctuate with the market, a Fixed Indexed Annuity **protects** the full amount that you contribute.

To help you understand the unique properties of an indexed investment, it helps to break the investment down according to these terms:

- *Equity* refers to the amount of money you will put into the annuity. For example, if you have $150,000 saved in a 401(k), and you want to restructure that for a portion of your retirement income, your *equity* would be $150,000.
- *Indexed* refers to how the annuity is keyed. It may be keyed to the S&P 500 or the Dow Jones Industrial Average or any number of indices. This is how the percentage on your rate of return is calculated. Although keyed to the market, FIAs are considered a Safe Money option because they have a guaranteed principal, meaning you can't lose money in this investment due to market loss.
- *Annuity* refers to the annual payout of an income.

When purchased with an income rider, FIAs can offer the income dependability of a pension-like investment, controlled and administered by you. You choose the amount of money you put in, when to turn on the income stream, and for how long. They offer guaranteed principal, tax-deferred growth, lifetime income options and potentially money to your beneficiaries.

WHY INDEXED ANNUITIES RETAIN THEIR GAIN

When you put your money into an annuity, you are essentially buying an investment product from an insurance company. It is a contract between you and the insurance company that provides the investment tool. Let's say you have saved $100,000 and need it to generate income to meet your needs above and beyond your

Social Security and pension checks. You give the $100,000 to an insurance company, who in turn invests it to generate growth.

They usually select investments that have modest returns over long term time horizons. In other words, they generally put it somewhere stable and predictable. Most commonly, they will invest it in a combination of bonds and treasuries that are safer and dependable ways to grow money. They use the money from the insurance products they sell to invest, use a portion of the returns to generate profits for themselves, and return a portion to clients in the form of payouts, claims, and structured income options.

As mentioned earlier, one of the most attractive qualities of these types of annuities is something called annual reset. Annual reset is sometimes also referred to as a "ratcheting." Instead of taking on the risk that comes with putting money in a fluctuating market, you can offset that risk onto the insurance company. It works like this: If the market goes down, you don't suffer a loss. Instead, the insurance company absorbs it. But if the market goes up, you share with the insurance company some of the profit made on the gain. The amount of gain you get is called your annuity participation rate. Typically the insurer will cap the amount of gain you can realize at somewhere between 3 and 7 percent. If the market goes up 10 percent, you would realize a portion of that gain (whatever percentage you are capped at). This means you will never lose money on your investment, while always gaining a portion of the upswings. The measurement period of your annuity can be calculated monthly, weekly and even daily, but most annuities are measured annually. The level of the index when you buy and the index level one year later will determine the amount of loss or gain. You and the insurance company are betting that the market will generally go up over time.

The graph below shows how the power of annual reset can work to protect your principal. The top line reflects the Income Rider Value of an account with an income rider attached. The value of this account can never drop, but you are never able to access this money except through regular income payments. There is also a fee for an income rider. The middle line, Accumulation Value, reflects the actual account value. This is money that you can access and this account can be emptied. If you elect to purchase an income rider and the actual account value drops to zero, you are still guaranteed your monthly income payments because FIAs purchased with income riders guarantee an income stream for life. The red line shows the performance of the S&P 500 over the same period of time.

HOW INCOME RIDERS WORK

One desirable optional feature with indexed annuities is the additional purchase of an income rider. Income riders are designed to provide safety of principal and a guaranteed lifetime income to people who are worried about running out of money during retirement. Here is how they work:

When you use that $100,000 to buy a contract with an insurance company in the form of an annuity, you are pegging your money on an index. It could be the S&P 500, the Dow Jones Industrial Average or any number of indexes. Because of the power of annual reset, you are able to retain the gains earned from the index of your choice when it goes up, without losing principal when the index goes down.

To generate income from the annuity, you select something called an income rider. Essentially, the income rider creates a separate account which shows a different rate of growth from which the insurance company will pay you an income while you have your money in their annuity. Your income rider account is a larger number than what your investment is actually worth, and if you select the income rider, it will increase in value over time, providing you with more income. As mentioned earlier, you do not have access to the income account value because this is essentially an

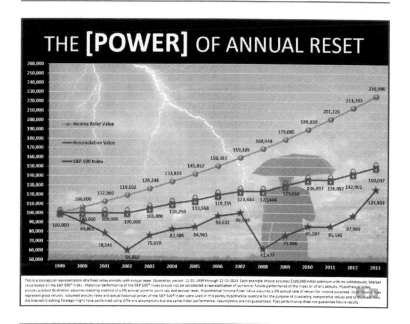

annuitized stream. Your actual money and the money you DO have access to is still in the regular account. As the insurance company holds your money and invests it, they generate a return on it that they use to pay you a regular monthly income based on the higher number of the account created by the income rider. The insurance company has to outperform the amount that they pay you in order to make a profit.

Remember, insurance companies make long-term investments that provide them with predictable flows of money. They like to stabilize the amount of money that goes in and out of their doors instead of paying and receiving large unpredictable chunks at once. When you opt for an income rider, an insurance company can reliably predict how much money they will pay out to you over a set period of time. It's predictable, and they like that. They can base their business on those predictable numbers.

In order to encourage investors to leave their money in their annuity contracts, insurance companies create surrender periods that protect their investments. If you remove your money from the annuity contract during the surrender period, you will pay a penalty and will not be able to receive your entire investment amount back. A typical surrender period is 10 years. If after three years you decide that you want your $100,000 back, the insurance company has that money tied up in bonds and other investments with the understanding that they will have it for another seven years. Because they will take a hit on removing the money from their investments prematurely, you will have to pay a surrender charge that makes up for their loss. During the surrender period, an annuity is not a demand deposit account like a savings or checking account. The higher returns that you are guaranteed from an annuity are dependent on the timeframe you selected. The longer an insurance company can hold your money, the easier it is for them to guarantee a predictable return on it.

If you leave your money in the annuity contract, you get a reliable monthly income no matter what happens in the market. **Once the surrender period has expired, you can remove your money whenever you want.** Your money becomes liquid again because the insurance company has used it in an investment that fit the timeline of your surrender period. For many people, this is an attractive trade off that can provide a creative solution for filling their income gap.

When is an annuity with an income rider right for you? A good financial professional can help you make that determination by taking the time to listen closely to your situation and understanding what your needs are as you enter retirement. Every salesperson has a bag full of brochures and PowerPoint presentations, but they need to know exactly what the financial concerns of their individual clients are in order to help them make the most informed and beneficial decision. Some people need income today, others need it in five or 10 years. Others may have their income needs met but are planning to move closer to their children and will need to buy a house in 10 years. Or, if you want income in 15 years, you might want to choose a different investment product for 10 years, and then switch to an annuity with an income rider during the last five years of your timeline. Everyone's situation is different and everyone's needs are different.

OTHER BENEFITS: CRITICAL CARE RIDERS

Just like an income rider, a critical care rider can be added to your annuity at the time of its purchase. Adding this type of rider to your annuity can provide you or your spouse with an income doubler should one of you need to fund the cost of long term care during your lifetime. Living benefits is another term for a type of benefit that can increase your income during a health-care related need. Living Benefits provide you with money while you are still alive to cover the expense of home health care and long term care. Many newer annuity policies being offered by life insurance companies come with benefits that can double the income of the policy holder to cover the cost of health care. Living Benefits on a life insurance policy may be harder to qualify for and are dependent on your health history.

Annuities come in a variety of shapes and sizes. Finding the right one for you will take a conversation with your financial professional. Be sure you fully understand the features, benefits and costs of any annuity you are considering before investing money.

CREATING AN INCOME PLAN

Creating an income plan before you retire allows you to satisfy your need for lifetime income and ensures that your lifestyle can last as long as you do. You also want to create a plan that operates in the most efficient way possible. Doing so will give you more security and peace of mind, and will potentially allow you to build your legacy down the road.

Using annuities for income generation includes the following steps:

- Review your income needs and look specifically at the shortfall you may have during each year of your retirement based on your Social Security income, and income from any other assets you have.
- Ask yourself where you are in your payout or income phase. Is retirement one year away? 10 years away? Last year?
- Determine how much money you need and how you need to structure your existing assets to provide for that need.
- If you have an asset from which you need to generate income, consider options offered by purchasing an income rider on an annuity.

CHAPTER 5 RECAP //

- After Social Security and your additional income are accounted for, the amount that's left to meet your needs is called the *Income Gap*. It's important to find the right investment tool for filling the income gap, because most retirees will live longer than their parents did.
- Today's new annuities can give you a guaranteed lifetime income without annuitization. Annuities with income riders give you both guaranteed income and control of your principal. The income can go up in value as you wait to trigger a monthly check.
- Although an annuity is an income-producing asset that does not subject your income to market risk, it still has the opportunity to grow. Indexed annuities such as the Fixed Indexed Annuity (FIA) participate in market growth without market loss through a strategy known as indexing. Indexing combined with the power of annual reset gives you both growth and the guaranteed safety of your principal.
- The benefits of an FIA include: guarantee of principal, a minimum guaranteed cash value, no fees, access to your money, bonus money, tax deferral, and a guaranteed lifetime income.
- Be sure you understand the features, benefits, costs and fees associated with any annuity product before you invest.

6

WHAT IS YELLOW MONEY?

Once you have worked with a financial professional to structure your income needs, it's time to take a look at the future. With your immediate income needs met, you have the opportunity to take your additional assets and leverage them for profit to supplement your income in the future, to prepare for anticipated health care costs or to contribute to your legacy. Stable income also means that you should have the staying power to stick with your investment portfolio through the ups and downs in the market.

> » *Paul is 69 years old. He retired four years ago. He relied on income from an IRA for three years in order to increase his Social Security benefit. He also made significant investments in 36 different mutual funds. He chose to diversify among the funds by selecting a portion for growth, another for good dividends, another that focused on promising small cap*

companies and a final portion that works like index funds. All the money that Paul had in mutual funds he considered accumulation money that he wanted to rely on in his 80s. After the stock market took a hit in 2008, Paul lost some confidence in his investments and decided to sit down with a financial professional to see if his portfolio was able to recover.

The professional Paul met with was able to determine what goals he had in mind. Specifically, the financial professional determined what Paul actually wanted and needed the money for, and when he needed it. His professional also looked inside each of the mutual funds and discovered several instances of overlap. While Paul had created diversity in his portfolio by selecting funds focused on different goals, he didn't account for overlap in the companies in which the funds were invested. Out of the 36 funds, his professional found that 20 owned nearly identical stock. While most of the companies were good investments, the high instance of overlap did not contribute to the healthy investment diversity that Paul wanted. Paul's financial professional also provided him with a report that explained the concentration ratio of his holdings (noting how much of his portfolio was contained within the top 25 stock holdings), the percentage of his portfolio that each company in which he invested in represented (showing the percentage of net assets that each company made up as an overall position in his portfolio) and the portfolio date of his account (showing when the funds in his portfolio were last updated: as funds are required to report updates only twice per year, it was possible that some of his fund reports could be six months old).

Paul's professional consolidated his assets into one invest-ment management strategy. This allowed Paul's investments to be managed (Yellow) by someone he trusted who knew his specific investment goals and needs. Eliminating redundancy and overlap in his portfolio was easy to do but difficult to detect since Paul had multiple funds with multiple brokerage firms. Paul sat down with a professional to see if his mutual funds could perform well, and he left with a consolidated management plan and a money manager that understood him personally. That's Yellow Money at its best.

The money you have left after you've calculated your income needs has the potential of becoming Red Money: your stocks, mutual funds and other investment products that you want to continue accumulating value with the market. You now have the luxury of taking a closer second look at your Red Money to determine how you would like to manage it.

As we talked about earlier, the risk inherent in managing your Red Money is very real and could have a lasting impact on your assets. So, how much of your Red Money do you invest, and in what kinds of markets, investment products and stocks do you invest? There are a lot of different directions in which you can take your money. One thing is for sure: significant accumulation depends on investing in the market. How you go about doing it is different for everyone. Gathering stocks, bonds and investment funds together in a portfolio without a cohesive strategy behind them could cause you to miss out on the benefits of a more thoughtful and planful approach. The end result is that you may never really understand what your money is doing, where and how it is really invested, and which investment principles are behind the investment products you hold. While you may have goals for each individual piece of your portfolio, it is likely that you don't have a comprehensive plan for your Red Money, which may mean that *you might be taking on more risk than you would like, and are getting less return for it than is possible.*

Enter *Yellow Money.* **YELLOW Money is money that is managed by a professional *with a purpose.*** After your income needs are met and you have assets that you would like to dedicate to accumulation, there are decisions you need to make about how to invest those assets. You can buy stocks, index funds, mutual funds, bonds — you name it — you can invest in it. However, the difference between Hope So Red Money and Yellow Money is that Yellow Money has a cohesive strategy behind it that is *implemented by a professional*. When you manage your Red Money with an investment plan, it becomes Yellow Money: *money that is being managed with a specific purpose, a specific set of focused goals and a specific strategy in mind.* Yellow Money is still a type of Red Money and it comes with different levels of risk. But Yellow Money is under the watchful eye of professionals who have a stake in the success of your money in the market and who can recommend a range of strategies from those designed for preservation to those targeting rapid growth. You don't want to miss out on achieving the right level of risk, and more importantly, composing a careful plan for the return of your assets.

It can be helpful to think of Red Money and Yellow Money using this analogy:

If you needed to travel through an unfamiliar city in a foreign country, you could rent a car or perhaps hire a driver. Were you to drive yourself, you would try to gain guidance from perplexing road signs and need to adhere to traffic rules—with no experience or assistance to lean on. It would take longer to get to where you want to go, and the chance of a traffic accident would be higher. If you hired a driver, they would manage your journey. A driver would know the route, how to avoid traffic, and follow the rules of the road.

Red Money is like driving yourself. With Yellow Money, you are still traveling by car, but now you have a professional working on your behalf.

TAKING A CLOSER LOOK AT YOUR PORTFOLIO

Think about your investment portfolio. Think specifically of what you would consider your Red Money. Do you know what is there? You may have several different investment products like individual mutual funds, bond accounts, stocks, and alternative investments. You may have inherited a stock portfolio from a relative, or you might be invested in a bond account offered by the company for which you worked due to your familiarity with them. While you may or may not be managing your investments individually, the reality is that you probably don't have an overall management strategy for all of your investments. Investments that aren't Yellow are simply Red Money, or money that is at risk in the market.

Harnessing the earning potential of your Red Money relies on more than a collection of stocks and bonds, however. It needs guided management. A good money manager uses the knowledge they have about the level of risk with which you are comfortable, what you need or want to use your money for, when you want or need it and how you want to use it. The Yellow Money investments that they choose for you will still have a certain level of risk, but under the right management, control and process, you have a far better chance of a successful outcome that meets your specific needs.

When you sit down with an investment professional, you can look at all of your assets together. Chances are that you have accumulated a number of different assets over the last 20, 30 or 50 years. You may have a 401(k), an IRA, a Roth IRA, an account of self-directed stocks, a brokerage account, etc. Wherever you put your money, a financial professional will go through your assets and help you determine the level of risk to which you are exposed now and should be exposed in the future.

AVOIDING EMOTIONAL INVESTING

There's no way around it; people get emotional about their money. And for good reason. You've spent your life working for it, exchanging your time and talent for it, and making decisions about how to invest it, save it and make it grow. The maintenance of your lifestyle and your plans for retirement all depend on it. The best investment strategies, however, don't rely on emotions. One of Yellow Money's greatest strengths lies in the fact that it is managed by someone who understands your needs and desires, but doesn't make decisions about your money under the influence of emotion.

A well-managed Yellow investment account meets your goals as a whole, not in individualized and piecemeal ways. Professional money managers do this by creating requirements for each type of investment in which they put your money. We'll call them "screens." Your money manager will run your holdings through the screens they have created to evaluate different types of investment strategies. A professionally managed Yellow account will only have holdings that meet the requirements laid out in the overall management plan that was designed to meet your investment goals. The holdings that don't make it through the screens, the ones that don't contribute to your investment goals, are sold and the proceeds redistributed to investments that your financial professional has determined to be appropriate.

Different screens apply to different Yellow Money strategies. For example, if one of your goals is significant growth, which would require taking on more risk alongside the potential for more return, an investment professional would screen for companies that have high rates of revenue and sales growth, high earnings growth, rising profit margins, and innovative products. On the other hand, if you want your portfolio to be used for income, which would call for lower risk and less return, your professional would screen for dividend yield and sector diversification. *Every investor has a different goal, and every goal requires a customized strategy that uses quantitative screens.* A professional will create a portfolio that reflects your investment desires. If some of the current assets you own complement the strategies that your professional recommends, those will likely stay in your portfolio.

Screening your assets removes emotions from the equation. It removes attachment to underperforming or overly risky investments. Financial professionals aren't married to particular stocks or mutual funds for any reason. They go by the numbers and see your portfolio through a lens shaped by your retirement goals. Your professional understands your wants and needs, and creates an investment strategy that takes your life events and future plans into account. It's a planful approach, and it allows you to tap into the tools and resources of a professional who has built a career around successful investing. Managing money is a full-time job and is best left to a professional money manager.

Removing emotions from investing also allows you to be unaffected by the day-to-day volatility of the market. Your financial professional doesn't ask where the market is going to be in a year, three years or a month from now. If you look at the value of the stock market from the beginning of the twentieth century to today, it's going up. Despite the Great Depression, despite the 1987 crash, despite the 2008 market downturn, the market, as a whole, trends up. Remember the major market downturn in 2008 when the market lost 30 percent of its value? Not only did it completely recover, it has far exceeded its 2008 value. Emotional investing led countless people to sell low as the market went down, and buy the same shares back when the market started to recover. That's an expensive way to do business. While you can't afford to lose money that you need in two, three or five years, your Need Later Money has time to grow. One way to do so is to make it Yellow Money.

CREATING AN INVESTMENT STRATEGY

Just like Paul in our previous story examples, chances are that you can benefit from taking a more Yellow investment approach tailored to your goals. Yellow Money is generally money that you don't need to rely on for income that you want to grow for needs you'll have in at least 10 years. You can work with your financial planner to create investments that meet your needs within different timeframes. You may need to rely on some of your Yellow Money in 10, 15 or 20 years, whether for additional income, a large purchase you plan on making or a vacation. Whatever you want it for, you will need it down the road. A financial professional can help you rescale the risk to your assets as they grow, helping you lock in your profits and secure a source of income you can depend on later.

So what does a Yellow Money account look like? Here's what it *doesn't* look like: a portfolio with 49 small cap mutual funds, a dozen individual stocks and an assortment of bond accounts. A brokerage account with a hodgepodge of investments, even if goal-oriented, is not a professionally managed Yellow account. It's still Red Money. Remember, Yellow Money is an account overseen by a professional that has an overarching investment philosophy. When you look at making investments that will perform to meet your future income needs, the burning question becomes: How much should you have in the market and how should it be invested? Working with a professional will help you determine how much risk you should take, how to balance your assets so they will meet your goals and how to plan for the big ticket items, like health care expenses, that may be in your future. Yes, Yellow Money is exposed to risk, but by working with a professional, you can manage that risk in a productive way.

WHY YELLOW MONEY?

If you have met your immediate income needs for retirement, why bother with professionally managing your other assets? The money you have accumulated above and beyond your income needs probably has a greater purpose. It may be for your children or grandchildren. You may want to give money to a charity or organization that you admire. In short, you may want to craft your legacy. It would be advantageous to grow your assets in the best manner possible. A financial professional has built a career around managing money in profitable ways. They are experts under the supervision of the organization that they represent.

Turning to Yellow Money also means that you don't have to burden yourself with the time commitment, the stress, and the cost of determining how to manage your money. Yellow Money can help you better enjoy your retirement. Do you want to sit down in your home office every day and determine how to best allocate your assets, or do you want to be living your life while someone else manages your money for you? When the majority of your Red Money is Yellow with a specific purpose managed by a financial professional, you don't have to be worrying about which stocks to buy and sell today or tomorrow.

SEEKING FINANCIAL ADVICE: STOCK BROKERS VS. INVESTMENT ADVISOR REPRESENTATIVES

Investors basically have access to two types of advice in today's financial world: advice from stock brokers and advice given by investment advisors. Most investors, however, don't know the difference between types of advice and the people from whom they receive advice. Today, there are two primary types of advice offered to investors: advice given by a commission-based registered representative (brokers) and advice given by fee-based Investment Advisor Representatives. Unfortunately, many investors are not aware that a difference exists; nor have they been explained the distinction between the two types of advice. In a survey taken by TD Ameritrade, the top reasons investors choose to work with an independent registered investment advisor are:*

- Registered Investment Advisors are required, as fiduciaries, to offer advice that is in the best interest of clients
- More personalized service and competitive fee structure offered at a Registered Investment Advisor firm
- Dissatisfaction with full commission brokers

The truth is that there is a great deal of difference between stock brokers and investment advisor representatives. For starters, investment advisor representatives are obligated to act in an investor's best interests in all aspects of a financial relationship. Confusion continues to exist among investors struggling to find the best financial advice out there and the most credible sources of advice.

Here is some information to help clear up the confusion so you can find good advice from a professional you can trust:

- Investment advisor representatives have the fiduciary duty to act in a client's best interest at all times with every investment decision they make. Stock brokers and brokerage firms usually do not act as fiduciaries to their investors and are not obligated to make decisions that are entirely in the best interest of their customers. For example, if you decide you want to invest in precious metals, a stock broker would offer you a precious metals account from their firm. An Investment Advisor would find you a precious metals account that is the best fit for you based on the investment strategy of your portfolio.

---

*2011 Advisor Sentiment Study, commissioned by TD AMERITRADE. TD Ameritrade, Inc.

- Investment advisors give their clients a Form ADV describing the methods that the professional uses to do business. An Investment Advisor also obtains client consent regarding any conflicts of interest that could exist with the business of the professional.
- Stock brokers and brokerage firms are not obligated to provide comparable types of disclosure to their customers.
- Whereas stock brokers and firms routinely earn large profits by trading as principal with customers, Investment Advisors cannot trade with clients as principal (except in very limited and specific circumstances).
- Investment Advisors charge a pre-negotiated fee with their clients in advance of any transactions. They cannot earn additional profits or commissions from their customers' investments without prior consent. Registered Investment Advisors are commonly paid an asset-based fee that aligns their interests with those of their clients. Brokerage firms and stock brokers, on the other hand, have much different payment agreements. Their revenues may increase regardless of the performance of their customers' assets.
- Unlike brokerage firms, where investment banking and underwriting are commonplace, Registered Investment Advisors must manage money in the best interests of their customers. Because Registered Investment Advisors charge set fees for their services, their focus is on their client. Brokerage firms may focus on other aspects of the firm that do not contribute to the improvement of their clients' assets.
- Unlike brokers, Registered Investment Advisors do not get commissions from fund or insurance companies for selling their investment products.

Just to drive home the point, here is what a fiduciary duty to a client means for a Registered Investment Advisor. Registered Investment Advisors must:*

- Always act in the best interest of their client and make investment decisions that reflect their goals.
- Identify and monitor securities that are illiquid.
- When appropriate, employ fair market valuation procedures.
- Observe procedures regarding the allocation of investment opportunities, including new issues and the aggregation of orders.
- Have policies regarding affiliated broker-dealers and maintenance of brokerage accounts.
- Disclose all conflicts of interest.
- Have policies on use of brokerage commissions for research.
- Have policies regarding directed brokerage, including step-out trades and payment for order flow.
- Abide by a code of ethics.

*2011 Advisor Sentiment Study, commissioned by TD AMERITRADE. TD Ameritrade, Inc.

CHAPTER 6 RECAP //

- Yellow Money is money that is Yellow by a professional with a purpose. It is still considered a type of Red Money, but there is a dedicated direction, strategy and end goal in mind, which makes it less dangerous.
- Red Money is like driving yourself in unfamiliar territory. With Yellow Money, you are still traveling by car, but now you have a professional driving on your behalf.
- Yellow Money is Yellow without emotions. A financial professional qualified to manage Yellow money uses specific criteria designed to fit into your overall financial plan so that it works the way you want it to.

7

HOW WILL THE STOCK MARKET IMPACT YOUR RETIREMENT?

Virginia lives next door to George and Dee Weston and worked for a manufacturing company for 34 years. During her time there, she acquired bonuses and pay raises that often included shares of stock in the company. She also dedicated part of her paycheck every month to a 401(k) that bought stock in the company. By the time she retired, Virginia had $250,000 worth of company stock.

Although she had contributed to her 401(k) account every month, Virginia didn't cultivate any other assets that could generate income for her during retirement. Virginia also retired early at age 62 because of her failing health. The commute to work every day was becoming difficult in her weakened condition and she wanted to enjoy the rest of her life in retirement instead of working in the cramped office of the restaurant supply company.

Because she retired early, Virginia failed to maximize her Social Security benefit. While she lives a modest lifestyle, her income needs are $3,500 per month. Virginia's monthly Social Security check only covers $1,900, leaving her with a $1,600 income gap. To supplement her Social Security check, Virginia sells $1,600 of company stock each month to meet her income needs. A $250,000 401(k) is nothing to sneeze at, but reducing its value by $1,600 every month will decimate her savings within 10 years. And that's if the market stays neutral or grows modestly. If the market takes a downturn, the money that Virginia relies on to fill her income gap will rapidly diminish. Even if the market starts going up in a couple of years, it will take much larger gains for her to recover the value that she lost due to the math of rebounds (which will be explained shortly).

Unhappily for Virginia, she retired in 2007, just before the major market downturn that lasted for several years. She lost more than 20 percent of the value of her stock. Because Virginia needed to sell her stock to meet her basic income needs, the market price of the stock was secondary to her need for the money. When she needed money, she was forced to sell however many shares she needed to fill her income gap that month. And if she has a financial crisis, involving a need for long term medical care, for example, she will be forced to sell stock even if the market is low and her shares are nearly worthless.

Virginia realizes that she could have relied on an investment structured to deliver her a regular income while protecting the value of her investment. She could have kept her $250,000 from diminishing while enjoying her lifestyle into retirement regardless of the volatility of the market. Ideally, Virginia would have restructured her 401(k) to reflect the level of risk that she was able to take. In her case, she would have had most of her money in Green Money assets, allowing her to rely on the value of her assets when she needed them.

MATH OF REBOUNDS

Taking a hit in the market hurts no matter how large your nest egg is, but most people don't realize that it requires an even larger step forward to return to where you were once you take that step back. After a loss, your money isn't growing and earning the same way it was before the hit occurred. The math of rebounds, as it is known, uses the percentage of the investment, and not the dollar amount, to calculate what you will need to earn in order to recapture your losses.

For example, if you had $100,000 invested in the stock market in 2007, and along comes the downturn of 2008, the market takes a reduction of 50 percent. So now your $100,000 becomes $50,000. What has to happen for us to get back up to $100,000? It took a 50 percent loss to lose $50,000 but it will take a 100 percent gain to get your account back to where you were before. This is why we advocate securing the money you need for income first, because exposing your nest egg to a stock market loss during the years near retirement can have lasting and devastating effects.

SEQUENCE OF RETURNS

Whether the market is high or low at the time of your retirement is another thing that's out of your control, yet it can have a big impact on the comfort of your retirement years. Most people don't realize that it's the *sequence of returns* that influences the value of your account even more than the *actual rate of return*.

Imagine two retirees with the same starting balance of $500,000. Retiree A is 66 years old and drawing 5 percent on that balance for income with an average rate of return of 8.43 percent.

Year One: the market is up by 31.69 percent
Year Two: market is down by 3.11 percent
Year Three: market is up by 30.47 percent
Year Four: market is up by 7.62 percent.

This continues for 20 years. At the age of 85, Retiree A sees a market loss of 37 percent, but because of the sequence of returns, **his account balance is a happy and healthy $1,537,593.**

Retiree B, on the other hand, sees that big drop right away, in year one. We can use the exact same starting balance of $500,000, the same withdrawal rate of 5 percent, and the same average rate of return of 8.43 percent. **The only difference is we will reverse the sequence of the returns.**

Year One: the market is down by 37 percent
Year Two: the market is up by 5.49 percent
Year Three: the market is up by 15.84 percent
Year Four, the market is up by 4.91 percent.

This continues for 20 years. At the age of 85, investor B sees a market gain of 31.69 percent, but because of the sequence of returns, **his account balance is a tragic and dismal $0.00.**

HOW REAL PEOPLE MAKE INVESTMENT DECISIONS

It can be challenging to watch the stock market's erratic changes every month, week or even every day. When you have your money riding on it, the ride can feel pretty bumpy. When you are managing your money by yourself, emotions inevitably enter into the mix. The Dow Jones Industrial Average and the S&P 500 represent more to you than market fluctuations. They represent your retirement dreams. It's hard not to be emotional about it.

Everyone knows you should buy low and sell high. But this is what is more likely to happen:

The market takes a downturn, similar to the 2008 crash, and investors see as much as a 30 percent loss in their stock holdings. It's hard to watch, and it's harder to bear the pain of losing that much money. The math of rebounds means that they will need to rely on even larger gains just to get back to where things were before the downturn. They sell. But eventually, and inevitably, the market begins to rise again. Maybe slowly, maybe with some moderate growth, but by the time the average investor notices an upward trend and wants to buy in again, they have already missed a great deal of the gains.

EMOTIONS AND YOUR MONEY

In 2013, DALBAR, the well-respected financial services market research firm, released their annual "Quantitative Analysis of Investment Behavior" report (QAIB). The report studied the impact of market volatility on individual investors: people like Virginia, or anyone who was managing (or mismanaging) their own investments in the stock market.

According to the study, volatility not only caused investors to make decisions based on their emotions, those decisions also harmed their investments and prevented them from realizing potential gains. So why do people meddle so much with their investments when the market is fluctuating? Part of the reason is that many people have financial obligations that they don't have control over. Significant expenses like house payments, the unexpected cost of replacing a broken-down car, and medical bills can put people in a position where they need money. If they need to sell investments to come up with that money, they don't have the luxury of selling when they *want* to. They must sell when they *need* to.

DALBAR's "Quantitative Analysis of Investor Behavior" has been used to measure the effects of investors' buying, selling and mutual fund switching decisions since 1994. The QAIB shows time and time again over nearly a 20 year period that the average investor earns less, and in many cases, significantly less than the performance of mutual funds suggests. QAIB's goal is to improve independent investor performance and to help financial profes-

sionals provide helpful advice and investment strategies that address the concerns and behaviors of the average investor.

An excerpt from the report claims that:*

*"QAIB offers guidance on how and where investor behaviors can be
improved. No matter what the state of the mutual fund industry,
boom or bust: Investment results are more dependent on investor
behavior than on fund performance. Mutual fund investors who hold
on to their investments are more successful than those who time the
market.*

*QAIB uses data from the Investment Company Institute (ICI),
Standard & Poor's and Barclays Capital Index Products to compare
mutual fund investor returns to an appropriate set of benchmarks.*

*There are actually three primary causes for the chronic shortfall for
both equity and fixed income investors:*

1. *Capital not available to invest. This accounts for 25 percent
   to 35 percent of the shortfall.*
2. *Capital needed for other purposes. This accounts for 35 percent to 45 percent of the shortfall.*
3. *Psychological factors. These account for 45 percent to 55
   percent of the shortfall."*

**The key findings of Dalbar's QAIB report provide compelling
statistics about how individual investment strategies produced
negative outcomes for the majority of investors:**

- Psychological factors account for 45 percent to 55 percent
  of the chronic investment return shortfall for both equity
  and fixed income investors.
- Asset allocation is designed to handle the investment
  decision-making for the investor, which can materially
  reduce the shortfall due to psychological factors.

---

*2013 QAIB, Dalbar, March 2013

- Successful asset allocation investing requires investors to act on two critical imperatives:
  1. Balance capital preservation and appreciation so that they are aligned with the investor's objective.
  2. Select a qualified allocator.
- The best way for an investor to determine their risk tolerance is to utilize a risk tolerance assessment. However, these assessments must be accessible and usable.
- Evaluating allocator quality requires analysis of the allocator's underlying investments, decision-making-process and whether or not past efforts have produced successful outcomes.
- Choosing a top allocator makes a significant difference in the investment results one will achieve.
- Mutual fund retention rates suggest that the average investor has not remained invested for long enough periods to derive the potential benefits of the investment markets.
- Retention rates for asset allocation funds exceed those of equity and fixed income funds by over a year.
- Investors' ability to correctly time the market is highly dependent on the direction of the market. Investors generally guess right more often in up markets. However, in 2012 investors guessed right only 42 percent of the time during a bull market.
- Analysis of investor fund flows compared to market performance further supports the argument that investors are unsuccessful at timing the market. Market upswings rarely coincide with mutual fund inflows while market downturns do not coincide with mutual fund outflows.
- Average equity mutual fund investors gained 15.56 percent compared to a gain of 15.98 percent that just holding the S&P 500 produced.

- The shortfall in the long-term annualized return of the average mutual fund equity investor and the S&P 500 continued to decrease in 2012.
- The fixed-income investor experienced a return of 4.68 percent compared to an advance of 4.21 percent on the Barclays Aggregate Bond Index.
- The average fixed income investor has failed to keep up with inflation in nine out of the last 14 years.*

It doesn't take a financial services market research report to tell you that market volatility is out of your control. The report does prove, however, that before you experience market volatility, you should have an investment plan, and when the market is fluctuating, you should stand by your investment plan. You should also review and discuss your investment plan with your financial professional on a regular basis, ensuring he/she is aware of any changes in your goals, financial circumstances, your health or your risk tolerance. When the economy is under stress and the markets are volatile, investors can feel vulnerable. That vulnerability causes people to tinker with their portfolios in an attempt to outsmart the market. Financial professionals, however, don't try to time the market for their clients. They try to tap into the gains that can be realized by committing to long-term investment strategies.

*2013 QAIB, Dalbar, March 2013

CHAPTER 7 RECAP //

- The timing of market downturns is more critical to retirees than to the average investor. If you are making withdrawals on a market investment without principal guarantees, and the account suffers a loss, the math of rebounds dictates that rapid depletion of your funds will change what the future of your retirement looks like.

- The sequence of returns tells us that in addition to how the market performs, the order of those returns is just as important when it comes to calculating the value of your account.

- Emotions inevitably enter the mix during stock market downturns. According to the DALBAR "Quantitative Analysis of Investment Behavior" report released in 2013, the average fixed income investor managing their money alone failed to keep up with inflation in nine out of the last 14 years.

- Financial professionals don't try to outsmart the market when managing investments for their clients. Instead, they tap into the potential for gains by committing to proven and long-term investment strategies.

8
HOW TO MAKE THE RIGHT INVESTMENT CHOICES

Sam Weston Jr. is a corn and soybean farmer with 1,200 acres of land. He routinely retains somewhere between $40,000 and $80,000 in his checking and savings accounts. If a major piece of equipment fails and needs repair or replacement, Sam Jr. will need the money available to pay for the equipment and carry on with farming. If the price of feed for his cattle goes up one year, he will need to compensate for the increased overhead to his farming operation. He isn't a particularly wealthy farmer, but he has little choice but to keep a portion of money on hand in case something comes up and he must access it quickly. Most of his capital is held in livestock in the pasture or crops in the ground tied up for six to eight months of the year. When a major financial need arises, Sam Jr. can't just harvest 10 acres of *soybeans and use them for payment. He needs to depend heavily on liquidity in order to be a successful farmer.*

Old habits die hard, however, and when Sam Jr. finally hangs up his overalls and quits farming, he keeps his bank accounts flush with cash, just like in the old days. After selling the farm and the equipment, Sam Jr. keeps a huge portion of the profits in liquid investments because that's what he is familiar with. Unfortunately for Sam Jr., with his pile of money sitting in his checking account, he isn't even keeping pace with inflation. After all his hard work as a farmer, his money is losing value every day because he didn't shift to a paradigm of leveraging his assets to generate income and accumulate value.

Almost anything would be a better option for Sam Jr. than clinging to liquidity. He could have done something better to get either more return from his money or more safety, and at the very least would not have lost out to inflation.

Earlier we discussed how today's investment options require advice that is relevant to today. Traditional, outdated investment strategies are not only ineffective; they can be harmful to the average investor. One of the most traditional ways of thinking about investing is the risk versus reward trade-off. It goes something like this:

Investment options that are considered safer carry less risk, but also offer the potential for less return. Riskier investment options carry the burden of volatility and a greater potential for loss, but they also offer a greater potential for large rewards. Most professionals move their clients back and forth along this range, shifting between investments that are safer and investments that are structured for growth. Essentially, the old rules of investing dictate that you can either choose relative safety *or* return, but you can't have both.

Updated investment strategies work with the flexibility of liquidity to remake the rules. Here is how:

There are three dimensions that are inherent in any invest-ment: *Liquidity, Safety,* and *Return.* You can maximize any two of these dimensions at the expense of the third. If you choose Safety and Liquidity, this is like keeping your assets in a checking ac-count or savings account. This option delivers a lot of Safety and Liquidity, but at the expense of any Return. On the other hand, if you choose Liquidity and Return, meaning you have the potential for great return and can still reclaim your money whenever you choose, you will likely be exposed to a very high level of risk.

Understanding Liquidity can help you break the old Risk versus Safety trade-off. By identifying assets from which you don't require Liquidity, you can place yourself in a position to poten-tially profit from relatively safe investments that provide a higher than average rate of return.

Choosing Safety and Return over Liquidity can have signifi-cant impacts on the accumulation of your assets. In the case of Sam Jr., the paradigm shift from earning and saving to leveraging assets was a costly one.

THE NECESSITY OF AN EMERGENCY FUND

When the unexpected happens, what happens to your retirement income? If the heater in your car breaks or your roof needs replac-ing, you need to know where you can get the money without changing your income. Taking the funds from a qualified account might trigger a tax event; using the stock market to hold your emergency funds means you don't know with any certainty that the money will be there when you need it. While liquidity is the most essential component of an emergency fund, you also need to have some safety.

How much do you need to have in your emergency fund? The amount of an emergency fund can vary. We recommend having six months of daily expenses in a bank account you can access quickly and easily. If the need for liquidity goes above that amount, you can dip into your Yellow Money portfolio with no negative repercussions to your income. The money in your emergency account should be funds you can get to within 30 days or less and during retirement, these are *not* the funds you rely on for income.

CHOOSING THE RIGHT INVESTMENT TOOLS

How much Liquidity do you need? Think about it. If you haven't sat down and created an income plan for your retirement, your perceived need for Liquidity is a guess. You don't know how much cash you'll need to fill the income gap if you don't know the amount of your Social Security benefit or the total of your other income options.

If you *have* determined your income need and have made a plan for filling your income gap, you can partition your assets based on when you will need them. Using more than one investment tool is one way to achieve a balance between liquidity, safety and return. Both Red and Green Money investments come with different risks and different rewards depending on your individual income and growth needs. Today's newer, fixed indexed annuities can offer a way to achieve safety with a limited return and some liquidity if you don't need to access the money all at once. Securities offer access to liquidity with more aggressive growth but their safety is limited. Using both types of investments means you have a better chance of achieving balance.

With a comprehensive income plan in place, ***you can use new rules to enjoy both Safety and Return from your assets.***

CHAPTER 8 RECAP //

- The three aspects of any investment include liquidity, safety, and return. You can choose to maximize any two against the third.

- Choosing to maximize liquidity alone can be an expensive option because the sooner you need your money back, the less you can leverage it for safety and return. To plan for a successful retirement in today's economy requires a creative use of today's financial tools.

- A comprehensive income plan during retirement should include provisions for an emergency fund. This fund should be a liquid account you can readily access that is not connected to your retirement income.

9

TAXES AND HOW THEY IMPACT YOUR RETIREMENT

What is tax diversification?

Taxes play a starring role in the theater of retirement planning. Everyone is familiar with taxes (you've been paying them your entire working life), but not everyone is familiar with how to make tax planning a part of their retirement strategy.

Taxes are taxes, right? You'll pay them before retirement and you'll pay them during retirement. What's the difference? The truth is that a planful approach to taxes can help you save money, protect your assets and keep more of your retirement savings intact.

» *Darlene remarried at the age of 62, and entered into her retirement years with Paul, also a 62-year-old ready to retire. Paul takes Darlene to meet his financial professional in October. After structuring their assets to reflect their risk tolerance and creating assets that would provide them Green Money income during retirement, they feel good about their situation. They make decisions that allow them to maximize their Social Security benefits, they have plenty of options for filling their income gap, and earlier, Paul had begun a safe yet ambitious Yellow Money strategy with his professional. When their professional asks them about their tax plan, they tell him their CPA handled their taxes every year, and did a great job. Their professional says, "I don't mean who does your taxes, I mean, who does your tax planning?" Darlene and Paul aren't sure how to respond.*

Their professional brings Darlene and Paul's financial plan to the firm's CPA and has her run a tax projection for them. A week later their professional calls them with a tax plan for the year that will save them more than $3,000 on their tax return. The couple is shocked. A simple piece of advice from the CPA based on the numbers revealed that if they paid their estimated taxes before the end of the year, they would be able to itemize it as a deduction, allowing them to save thousands of dollars.

This solution won't work for everyone, and it may not work for Darlene and Paul every year. That's not the point. By being proactive with their approach to taxes and using the resources made available by their financial professional, they were able to create a tax plan that saved them money.

Tax *planning* **and** *tax* *reporting* **are two very different things.** Most people only *report* their taxes. March rolls around, people pull out their 1040s or use TurboTax to enter their income and taxable assets, and ship it off to Uncle Sam at the IRS. If you use a CPA to report your taxes, you are essentially paying them to record history. Doing your taxes in January, February, March or April means you are writing a history book. Planning your taxes in October, November or December means that you are writing the story as it happens. You can look at all the factors that are at play and make decisions that will impact your tax return *before* you file it.

You have the option of being proactive with your taxes and to plan for your future by making smart, informed decisions about how taxes affect your overall financial plan. When you retire, you move from the earning and accumulation phase of your life into the asset distribution phase of your life. For most people, that means relying on Social Security, a 401(k), an IRA, or a pension. Wherever you have put your Green Money for retirement, you are going to start relying on it to provide you with the income that once came as a paycheck. Most of these distributions will be considered income by the IRS and will be taxed as such. There are exceptions to that (not all of your Social Security income is taxed, and income from Roth IRAs is not taxed), but for the most part, your distributions will be subject to income taxes.

Working with a financial professional who, along with a CPA, makes recommendations about your finances to you, will keep you looking forward instead of in the rearview mirror as you enter retirement.

YOUR REQUIRED MINIMUM DISTRIBUTION

Regarding assets that you have in an IRA, when you reach 70 ½ years of age, you will be required to draw a certain amount of money from your IRA as income each year. That amount depends on your age and the balance in your IRA. The amount that you are required to withdraw as income is called a Required Minimum Distribution (RMD). Why are you required to withdraw money from your own account? Chances are the money in that account has grown over time, and the government wants to collect taxes on that growth. Failing to take your RMD comes with steep penalties. Ask your financial professional about what you need to do in order to avoid these penalties.

PLANNING FOR YOUR TAXES DURING RETIREMENT

When you retire, you move from the earning and accumulation phase of your life into the asset distribution phase of your life. For most people, that means relying on Social Security, a 401(k), an IRA, or a pension. Wherever you have put your Green Money for retirement, you are going to start relying on it to provide you with the income that once came as a paycheck. Most of these distributions will be considered income by the IRS and will be taxed as such. There are exceptions to that (not all of your Social Security income is taxed, and income from Roth IRAs is not taxed), but for the most part, your distributions will be subject to income taxes.

If you have a large balance in an IRA, there's a chance your RMD could increase your income significantly enough to put you into a higher tax bracket, subjecting you to a higher tax rate.

Here's where tax planning can really begin to work strongly in your favor. In the distribution phase of your life, you have a predictable income based on your RMDs, your Social Security benefit and any other income-generating assets you may have. What really impacts you at this stage is how much of that money you keep in your pocket after taxes. Essentially, *you will make more money saving on taxes than you will by making more money.* If you can reduce your tax burden by 30, 20 or even 10 percent, you earn yourself that much more money by not paying it in taxes.

How do you save money on taxes? By having a plan. In this instance, a financial professional can work with the CPAs at their firm to create a **distribution plan** that minimizes your taxes and maximizes your annual net income.

BUILDING A TAX DIVERSIFIED PORTFOLIO

So far so good: avoid taxes, maximize your net annual income and have a plan for doing it. When people decide to leverage the experience and resources of a financial professional, they may not be thinking of how distribution planning and tax planning will benefit their portfolios. Often more exciting prospects like planning income annuities, investing in the market and structuring investments for growth rule the day. Taxes, however, play a crucial role in retirement planning. Achieving those tax goals requires knowledge of options, foresight and professional guidance.

Finding the path to a good tax plan isn't always a simple task. Every tax return you file is different from the one before it because things constantly change. Your expenses change. Planned or unplanned purchases occur. Health care costs, medical bills, an inheritance, property purchases, reaching an age where your RMD kicks in or travel, any number of things can affect how much income you report and how many deductions you take each year.

Preparing for the ever-changing landscape of your financial life requires a tax-diversified portfolio that can be leveraged to balance the incomes, expenditures and deductions that affect you each year. A financial professional will work with you to answer questions like these:

- What does your tax landscape look like?
- Do you have a tax-diversified portfolio robust enough to adapt to your needs?
- Do you have a diversity of taxable and non-taxable income planned for your retirement?
- Will you be able to maximize your distributions to take advantage of your deductions when you retire?

- Is your portfolio strong enough and tax-diversified enough to adapt to an ever-changing (and usually increasing) tax code?

> *When Louise Weston's neighbor, Gloria, returns home after a week in the hospital recovering from a knee replacement, the 77-year-old calls her daughter, sister and her neighbor to let them know she is home and feeling well. She also should have called her CPA. Gloria's medical expenses for the procedure, her hospital stay, her medications and the ongoing physical therapy she attended amount to more than $50,000.*
>
> *Currently, Americans can deduct medical expenses that are more than 7.5 percent of their Adjusted Gross Income (AGI). Gloria's AGI is $60,000 the year of her knee replacement, meaning she is able to deduct $44,000 of her medical bills from her taxes that year. Her AGI dictated that she could deduct more than 80 percent of her medical expenses that year.* **Gloria didn't know this.**
>
> *Had she been working with a financial professional who regularly asked her about any changes in her life, her spending, or her expenses (expected or unexpected), Gloria could have saved thousands of dollars. Gloria can also file an amendment to her tax return to recoup the overpayment.*

This relatively simple example of how tax planning can save you money is just the tip of the iceberg. No one can be expected to know the entire U.S. tax code. But a professional who is working with a team of CPAs and financial professionals have an advantage over the average taxpayer who must start from square one on their own every year. Have you been taking advantage of all the deductions that are available to you?

PROACTIVE TAX PLANNING

The implications of proactive tax planning are far reaching, and are larger than many people realize. Remember, doing your taxes in January, February, March or April means you are writing a history book. Planning your taxes in October, November or December means that you are writing the story as it happens. You can look at all the factors that are at play and make decisions that will impact your tax return *before* you file it.

Realizing that tax planning is an aspect of financial planning is an important leap to make. When you incorporate tax planning into your financial planning strategy, it becomes part of the way you maximize your financial potential. Paying less in taxes means you keep more of your money. Simply put, the more money you keep, the more of it you can leverage as an asset. This kind of planning can affect you at any stage of your life. If you are 40 years old, are you contributing the maximum amount to your 401(k) plan? Are you contributing to a Roth IRA? Are you finding ways to structure the savings you are dedicating to your children's education? Do you have life insurance? Taxes and tax planning affects all of these investment tools. Having a relationship with a professional who works with a CPA can help you build a truly comprehensive financial plan that not only works with your investments, but also shapes your assets to find the most efficient ways to prepare for tax time. There may be years that you could benefit from higher distributions because of the tax bracket that you are in, or there could be years you would benefit from taking less. There may be years when you have a lot of deductions and years you have relatively few. **Adapting your distributions to work in concert with your available deductions** is at the heart of smart tax planning. Professional guidance can bring you to the next level of income distribution, allowing you to remain flexible enough to maximize your tax efficiency. And remember, saving money on taxes makes you more money than making money does.

What you have on paper is important: your assets, savings, and investments, which are financial expression of your work and time. It's just as important to know how to get it off the paper in a way that keeps most of it in your pocket. Almost anything that involves financial planning also involves taxes. Annuities, investments, IRAs, 401(k)s, 403(b), and many other investment options will have tax implications. Life also has a way of throwing curveballs. Illness, expensive car repair or replacement, or *any event that has a financial impact on your life will likely have a corresponding tax implication* around which you should adapt your financial plan. Tax planning does just that.

One dollar can end up being less than 25 cents to your heirs.

» *When Maggie's father passed away, she discovered that she was the beneficiary of her father's $500,000 IRA. Maggie has a husband, Frank, and three kids, Kyle, Ellie and Lizzie. She knew that her father had intended for her to pay off the house, with a large portion of the IRA to go toward funding the college educations of her three kids.*

After Maggie's father's estate is distributed, Maggie, who is 50 years old and whose oldest son and daughter are entering college, liquidates the IRA. By doing so, her taxable income for that year puts her in a 39.6 percent tax bracket, immediately reducing the value of the asset to $302,000. An additional 3.8 percent surtax on net investment income further diminishes the funds to $283,000. Liquidating the IRA in effect subjects much of Maggie's regular income to the surtax, as well. At this point, Maggie will be taxed at 43.4 percent. Maggie's state taxes are an additional 9 percent. Moreover, estate taxes on her father's assets claim another 22 percent.

By the time the IRS is through, Maggie's income from the IRA will be taxed at 75 percent, leaving her with $125,000

*of the original $500,000. After she pays off the existing
balance on her mortgage, Maggie and Frank are left with
$85,000. While it will help contribute to the education of
their kids, it wouldn't come anywhere near completely paying
for it, something the $500,000 could have easily done.*

As the above example makes clear, leaving an asset to your beneficiaries can be more complicated than it may seem. In the case of a
traditional IRA, after federal, estate and state taxes, the asset could
literally diminish to as little as 25 percent of its value.

How does working with a professional help you make smarter
tax decisions with your own finances? Any financial professional
worth their salt will be working with a firm that has a team of
trained tax professionals, including CPAs, who have an intimate
knowledge of the tax code and how to adapt a financial plan to it.

YELLOW MONEY AND TAXES

There are also tax implications for the money that you have managed professionally. People with portions of their investment portfolio that are actively traded can particularly benefit from having a
proactive tax strategy. Without going into too much detail, for tax
purposes there are two kinds of investment money: qualified and
non-qualified. Different investment strategies can have different
effects on how you are taxed on your investments and the growth
of your investments. Some are more beneficial for one kind of
investment strategy over another. Determining how to plan for
the taxation of non-qualified and qualified investments is fodder
for holiday party discussions at accounting firms. While it may
not be a stimulating topic for the average investor, you don't have
to understand exactly how it works in order to benefit from it.

While there are many differences between qualified and non-
qualified investments, the main difference is this: qualified plans
are designed to give investors tax benefits by deferring taxation of

their growth until they are withdrawn. Non-qualified investments are not eligible for these deferral benefits. As such, non-qualified investments are taxed whenever income is realized from them in the form of growth.

Actively and non-actively traded investments provide a simple example of how to position your investments for the best tax advantage. In an actively traded and managed portfolio, there is a high amount of buying and selling of stocks, bonds, funds, ETFs, etc. If that active portfolio of non-qualified investments does well and makes a 20 percent return one year and you are in the 39.6 percent tax bracket, your net gain from that portfolio is only about 12 percent (39.6 percent tax of the 20 percent gain is roughly 8 percent.) In a passive trading strategy, you can use a qualified investment tool, such as an IRA, to achieve 13, 14 or 15 percent growth (much lower than the actively traded portfolio), but still realize a higher net return because the growth of the qualified investment is not taxed until it is withdrawn.

Does this mean that you have to always rely on a buy and hold strategy in qualified investment tools? Not necessarily. The question is, if you have qualified and non-qualified investments, where do you want to position your actively traded and managed assets? Incorporating a planful approach to positioning your investments for more beneficial taxation can be done many ways, but let's consider one example. Keeping your actively managed investment strategies inside an IRA or some other qualified plan could allow you to realize the higher gains of those investments without paying tax on their growth every year. Your more passively managed funds could then be kept in taxable, non-qualified vehicles and methods, and because you aren't realizing income from them on an annual basis by frequently trading them, they grow sheltered from taxation.

If you are interested in taking advantage of tax strategies that maximize your net income, you need the attentive strategies, experience and knowledge of a professional who can give you options that position you for profit. At the end of the day, what's important to you as the consumer is how much you keep, your after-tax take home.

ESTATE TAXES

The government doesn't just tax your income from investments while you're alive. They will also dip into your legacy.

While estate taxes aren't as hot of a topic as they were a few years ago, they are still an issue of concern for many people with assets. While taxes may not apply on estates that are less than $5 million, certain states have estate taxes with much lower exclusion ratios. Some are as low as $600,000. Many people may have to pay a state estate tax. One strategy for avoiding those types of taxes is to move assets outside of your estate. That can include gifting them to family or friends, or putting them into an irrevocable trust. Life insurance is another option for protecting your legacy.

THE FUTURE OF U.S. TAXATION

Tax legislation over the course of American history has left one very resounding message: taxes go up.

The raising of the debt ceiling raised more than just the ability for our government to go further into debt. It also raised concerns and fears about the future of our economy. We are now seeing major swings in the markets with investors showing serious concerns over the future of investment valuations and their personal wealth.

Unfortunately, the general public is in a no-win situation for this solution to the problem. Printing money does not bode well for economic growth. This creates inflationary pressures that devalue the U.S. dollar and make everyone less wealthy. Cutting the entitlements that compose this liability leaves millions of people without benefits they have come to expect. The only other option, and one that the government knows all too well, is increasing taxes. In fact, according to a Congressional Budget Office paper issued in 2004:

"The term 'unfunded liability' has been used to refer to a gap between the government's projected financial commitment under a particular program and the revenues that are expected to be available to fund that commitment. But no government obligation can be truly considered 'unfunded' because of the U.S. government's sovereign power to tax—which is the ultimate resource to meet its obligations."

A balanced budget will be required at some point and with this will come higher taxes. We have uncertainty surrounding tax rates and how high they will go. Whether it is only on the top earners or unilaterally across all income levels is yet to be seen, but an increase of some sort will most certainly occur.

How do you prepare? Why spend so much time reassuring you that taxes will increase? Because you have an opportunity to take action. Now is the time to prepare for what will come and structure countermeasures for the good, the bad and the ugly of each of these legislative nightmares through tax-advantaged retirement planning.

You make more money by saving on taxes than you do by making more money. The simplistic logic of the statement makes sense when you discover it takes $1.50 in earnings to put that same dollar, saved in taxes, back in your pocket.

As simple as it sounds, it is much more difficult to execute. Most people fail to put together a plan as they near retirement, beginning with a simple cash flow budget. If you have not analyzed your proposed income streams and expenses, you could not possibly have taken the time to position these cash flows and other events into a tax-preferred plan.

Most people will state that they have a plan and, thus, do not need any further assistance in this area. The truth in most instances is that people could not show you their plan, and among the few that could, most would not be able to show you how they have executed it. In this regard, they might as well be Richard Nixon stating, "I am not a crook" for as much as they state, "I have a plan." The truth lies in waiting. As we approach or begin retirement, we should look at what cash flows we will have. Do we have a pension? How about Social Security? How much additional cash flow am I going to need to draw from my assets to maintain the lifestyle that I desire?

We spend our whole lives saving and accumulating wealth but spend so little time determining how to distribute this accumulation so as to retain it. We need to make sure we have the appropriate diversification of taxable versus non-taxable assets to complement our distribution strategy.

THE BENEFITS OF DIVERSIFICATION

Tax legislation over the course of American history has left one very resounding message: taxes go up.

Heading into retirement, we should be situated with a diversified tax landscape. The point to spending our whole lives accumulating wealth is not to see the size of the number on paper, but rather to be an exercise in how much we put in our pocket after removing it from the paper. To truly understand tax diversification, we must understand what types of money exist and how each of these will be treated during accumulation and, most importantly, during distribution. The following is a brief summary:

1. Free money
2. Tax-advantaged money
3. Tax-deferred money
4. Taxable money
    a. Ordinary income
    b. Capital gains and qualified dividends

FREE MONEY

Free money is the best kind of money regardless of tax treatment because, in the end, you have more money than you would have otherwise. Many employers will provide contributions toward employee retirement accounts to offer additional employment benefits and encourage employees to save for their own retirement. With this, employers often will offer a matching contribution in which they contribute up to a certain percentage of an employee's salary (generally three to five percent) toward that employee's retirement account when the employee contributes to their retirement account as well. For example, if an employee earns $50,000 annually and contributes three percent ($1,500) to their retirement account annually, the employer will also contribute three percent ($1,500) to the employee's account. That is $1,500 in free money. Take all you can get! Bear in mind that any employer contribution to a 401(k) will still be subject to taxation when withdrawn.

TAX-ADVANTAGED MONEY

Tax-advantaged money is the next best thing to free money. Although you have to earn tax-advantaged money, you do not have to give part of it away to Uncle Sam. Tax-advantaged money comes in three basic forms that you can utilize during your lifetime; four if prison inspires your future, but we are not going to discuss that option.

One of the most commonly known forms of tax-advantaged money is municipal bonds, which earn and pay interest that could be tax-advantaged on the federal level, or state level, or both. There are several caveats that should be discussed with regard to the notion of tax-advantaged income from municipal bonds. First, you will notice that tax-advantaged has several flavors from the state and federal perspective. This is because states will generally tax the interest earned on a municipal bond unless the bond is offered from an entity located within that state. This severely limits the availability of completely tax-advantaged municipal bonds and constrains underlying risk and liquidity factors. Second, municipal bond interest is added back into the equation for determining your modified adjusted gross income (MAGI) for Social Security. This could push your income above a threshold and subject a portion of your Social Security income to taxation.

In effect, if this interest subjects some other income to taxation then this interest is truly being taxed.

Last, municipal bond interest may be excluded from the regular federal tax system, but it is included for determining tax under the alternative minimum tax (AMT) system. In its basic form, the AMT system is a separate tax system that applies if the tax computed under AMT exceeds the tax computed under the regular tax system. The difference between these two computations is the alternative minimum tax.

TAX-ADVANTAGED MONEY: ROTH IRA

Roth accounts are probably the single greatest tax asset that has come from Congress outside of life insurance. They are well known but rarely used. Roth IRAs were first established by the Taxpayer Relief Act of 1997 and named after Senator William Roth, the chief sponsor of the legislation. Roth accounts are simply an account in the form of an individual retirement account or an employer sponsored retirement account that allows for tax-advantaged growth of earnings and, thus, tax-advantaged income.

The main difference between a Roth and a traditional IRA or employer-sponsored plan lies in the timing of the taxation. We are all very familiar with the typical scenario of putting money away for retirement through an employer plan, whereby they deduct money from our paychecks and put it directly into a retirement account. This money is taken out before taxes are calculated, meaning we do not pay tax on those earnings today. A Roth account, on the other hand, takes the money after the taxes have been removed and puts it into the retirement account, so we do pay tax on the money today. The other significant difference between these two is taxation during distribution in later years. Regarding our traditional retirement accounts, when we take the money out later it is added to our ordinary income and is taxed accordingly. Additionally, including this in our income subjects us to the consequences mentioned above for municipal bonds with Social Security taxation, AMT, as well as higher Medicare premiums. A Roth on the other hand is distributed tax-advantaged and does not contribute toward negative impact items such as Social Security taxation, AMT, or Medicare premium increases. It essentially comes back to us without tax and other obligations.

The best way to view the difference between the two accounts is to look at the life of a farmer. A farmer will buy seed, plant it in the ground, grow the crops and harvest it later for sale. Typically, the farmer would only pay tax on the crops that have been harvested and sold. But if you were the farmer, would you rather pay tax on the $5,000 of seed that you plant today or the $50,000 of crops harvested later? The obvious answer is $5,000 of seed today. The truth to the matter is that you are a farmer, except you plant dollars into your retirement account instead of seeds into the earth.

So why doesn't everyone have a Roth retirement account if things are so simple? There are several reasons, but the single greatest reason has been the constraints on contributions. If you earned over certain thresholds (MAGI over $125,000 single and $183,000 joint for 2012), you were not eligible to make contributions, and until last year, if your modified adjusted gross income (MAGI) was over $100,000 (single or joint), you could not convert a traditional IRA to a Roth. Outside these contribution limits, most people save for retirement through their employers and most employers do not offer Roth options in their plans.

The reason behind this is because Roth accounts are not that well understood and people have been educated to believe that saving on taxes today is the best possible course of action.

TAX-ADVANTAGED MONEY: LIFE INSURANCE

As previously mentioned, the single greatest tax asset that has come from Congress outside of life insurance is the Roth account. Life insurance is the little-known or little-discussed tax asset that holds some of the greatest value in your financial history both during life and upon death. It is by far the best tax-advantaged device available. We traditionally view life insurance as a way to protect our loved ones from financial ruin upon our demise and it should be noted that everyone who cares about someone should have life insurance. Purchasing a life insurance policy ensures that our loved ones will receive income from the life insurance company to help them pay our final expenses and carry on with their lives without us comfortably when we die. The best part of the life insurance windfall is the fact that nobody will have to pay tax on the money received. This is the single greatest tax-advantaged device available, but it has one downside, we do not get to use it. Only our heirs will.

The little known and discussed part of life insurance is the cash value build-up within whole life and universal life (permanent) policies. Life insurance is not typically seen as an investment vehicle for building wealth and retirement planning, although we should discuss briefly why this thought process should be re-evaluated. Permanent life insurance is generally misconceived as something that is very expensive for a wealth accumulation vehicle because there are mortality charges (fees for the death benefit) that detract from the available returns. Furthermore, those returns do not yield as much as the stock market over the long run. This is why many times you will hear the phrase "buy term and invest the rest," where "term" refers to term insurance.

Let us take a second to review two terms just used in regard to life insurance: term and permanent. Term insurance is an idea with which most people are familiar. You purchase a certain death benefit that will go to your heirs upon death and this policy will be in effect for a certain number of years, typically 10 to 20 years. The 10 to 20 years is the term of the policy and once you have reached that end you no longer have insurance unless you purchase another policy.

Permanent insurance on the other hand has no term involved. It is permanent as long as the premiums continue to be paid. Permanent insurance generally initially has higher premiums than term insurance for the same amount of death benefit coverage and it is this difference that is referred to when people say "invest the rest."

Simply speaking there are significant differences between these two policies that are not often considered when providing a comparative analysis of the numbers. One item that gets lost in the fray when comparing term and permanent insurance is that term usually expires before death. In fact, insurance studies show less than one percent of all term policies pay out death benefit claims. The issue arises when the term expires and the desire to have more insurance is still present.

A term policy with the same benefit will be much more expensive than the original policy and, many times, life events occur, such as cancer or heart conditions, which makes it impossible to acquire another policy and leaves your loved ones unprotected and tax-advantaged legacy planning out of the equation.

Another aspect and probably the most important piece in consideration of the future of taxation is the fact that permanent insurance has a cash accumulation value. Two aspects stand out with the cash accumulation value. First, as the cash accumulation value increases the death benefit will also increase whereas the death benefit for term insurance remains level and there is no cash accumulation. Second, the cash accumulation in a permanent policy offers value to you during your lifetime rather than to your heirs upon death. The cash accumulation value can be used for tax-advantaged income during your lifetime through policy loans. Most importantly, this tax-advantaged income is available during retirement for distribution planning, all while offering the same typical financial protection to your heirs.

TAX-DEFERRED MONEY

Tax-deferred money is the type of money with which most people are familiar, but we also briefly reviewed the idea above. Tax-deferred money is typically our traditional IRA, employer sponsored retirement plan or a non-qualified annuity. Essentially, you put money into an investment vehicle that will accumulate in value over time and you do not pay taxes on the earnings that grow these accounts until you distribute them. Once the money is distributed, taxes must be paid. However, the same negative consequences exist with regard to additional taxation and expense in other areas as previously discussed. The cash accumulation value can be used for tax-advantaged income.

TAXABLE MONEY

Taxable money is everything else and is taxable today, later or whenever it is received. These four types of money come down to two distinct classifications: taxable and tax-free. The greatest difference when comparing taxable and tax-advantaged income is a function of how much money we keep after tax. For help in determining what the differences should be, excluding outside factors such as Social Security taxation and AMT, a tax equivalent yield should be used.

TAX-ADVANTAGED IN THE REAL WORLD

To put the tax equivalent yield into perspective, let us look at an example: Bob and Mary are currently retired, living on Social Security and interest from investments and fall within the 25 percent tax bracket. They have a substantial portion of their investments in municipal bonds yielding 6 percent, which is quite comforting in today's market. The tax equivalent yield they would need to earn from a taxable investment would be 8 percent, a 2 percent gap that seems almost impossible given current market volatility. However, something that has never been put into perspective is that the interest from their municipal bonds is subject to taxation on their Social Security benefits (at 21.25 percent). With this, the yield on their municipal bonds would be 4.725 percent, and the taxable equivalent yield falls to 6.3 percent, leaving a gap of only 1.575 percent.

In the end, most people spend their lives accumulating wealth through the best, if not the only vehicle they know, a tax-deferred account. This account is most likely a 401(k) or 403(b) plan offered through our employer and may be supplemented with an IRA that was established at one point or another. As the years go by, people blindly throw money into these accounts in an effort to save for a retirement that we someday hope to reach.

The truth is, most people have an age selected for when they would like to retire, but spend their lives wondering if they will ever be able to actually quit working. To answer this question, you must understand how much money you will have available to contribute toward your needs. *In other words, you need to know what your after-tax income will be during this period.*

All else being equal, it would not matter if you put your money into a taxable, tax-deferred or tax-advantaged account as long as income tax rates never change and outside factors are never an event. The net amount you receive in the end will be the same.

Unfortunately, this will never be the case. We already know that taxes will increase in the future, meaning we will likely see higher taxes in retirement than during our peak earning years.

Regardless, saving for retirement in any form is a good thing as it appears from all practical perspectives that future government benefits will be cut and taxes will increase. You have the ability to plan today for efficient tax diversification and maximization of our after-tax dollars during your distribution years.

CHAPTER 9 RECAP //

- When you report your taxes, you are paying to record history. When you *plan* your taxes with a financial professional, you are proactively finding the best options for your tax return.

- At the age of 70 ½, the Federal Government requires all IRA participants to take their RMD, or Required Minimum Distribution. Failure to take your RMD can cost you thousands of dollars in taxes and penalty fees.

- Taxes play an important role during your retirement. It's important that you understand your obligations, and the differences between tax-deferred and tax-advantaged advantaged accounts.

- You make more money by saving on taxes than you do by making more money. This simple concept becomes extremely valuable to people in retirement and those living on fixed incomes.

- Tax planning can directly affect your beneficiaries, costing them or saving them hundreds of thousands of dollars.

10
THE BRANDEIS STORY

Louis Brandeis provides one of the best examples illustrating how tax planning works. Brandeis was Associate Justice on the Supreme Court of the United States from 1916 to 1939. Born in Louisville, Kentucky, Brandeis was an intelligent man with a touch of country charm. He described tax planning this way:

"I live in Alexandria, Virginia. Near the Court Chambers, there is a toll bridge across the Potomac. When in a rush, I pay the dollar toll and get home early. However, I usually drive outside the downtown section of the city and cross the Potomac on a free bridge.

The bridge was placed outside the downtown Washington, D.C. area to serve a useful social service—getting drivers to drive the extra mile and help alleviate congestion during the rush hour.

If I went over the toll bridge and through the barrier without paying a toll, I would be committing tax evasion.

If I drive the extra mile and drive outside the city of Washington to the free bridge, I am using a legitimate, logical and suitable method of tax avoidance, and I am performing a useful social service by doing so.

*The tragedy is that **few people know that the free bridge exists.** "*

Like Brandeis, most American taxpayers have options when it comes to "crossing the Potomac," so to speak. It's a financial planner's job to tell you what options are available. You can wait until March to file your taxes, at which time you might pay someone to report and pay the government a larger portion of your income. However, you could instead file before the end of the year, work with your financial professional and incorporate a tax plan as part of your overall financial planning strategy. Filing later is like crossing the toll bridge. Tax planning is like crossing the free bridge.

Which would you rather do?

The answer to this question is easy. Most people want to save money and pay less in taxes. What makes this situation really difficult in real life, however, is that the signs along the side of the road that direct us to the free bridge are not that clear. To normal Americans, and to plenty of people who have studied it, the U.S. tax code is easy to get lost in. There are all kinds of rules, exceptions to rules, caveats and conditions that are difficult to understand, or even to know about. What you really need to know is your options and the bottom line impacts of those options.

ROTH IRA CONVERSIONS

The attractive qualities of Roth IRAs may have prompted you to explore the possibility of moving some of your assets into a Roth account. Another important difference between the accounts is how they treat Required Minimum Distributions (RMDs). When you turn 70 ½ years old, you are required to take a minimum amount of money out of a traditional IRA. This amount is your

RMD. It is treated as taxable income. Roth IRAs, however, do not have RMDs, and their distributions are not taxable. Quite a deal, right?

While having a Roth IRA as part of your portfolio is a good idea, converting assets to a Roth IRA can pose some challenges, depending on what kinds of assets you want to transfer.

You may have heard about converting your IRA to a Roth IRA, but you might not know the full net result on your income. The main difference between the two accounts is that the growth of investments within a traditional IRA is not taxed until income is withdrawn from the account, whereas taxes are charged on contribution amounts to a Roth IRA, not withdrawals. The problem, however, is that when assets are removed from a traditional IRA, even if the assets are being transferred to a Roth IRA account, taxes apply.

There are a lot of reasons to look at Roth conversions. People have a lot of money in IRAs, up to multiple millions of dollars. Even with $500,000, when they turn 70 ½ years old, their RMD is going to be approximately $18,000, and they have to take that out whether they want to or not. It's a tax issue. Essentially, if you will be subject to high RMDs, it could have impacts on how much of your Social Security is taxable, and on your tax bracket.

By paying taxes now instead of later on assets in a Roth IRA, you can realize tax-advantaged growth. You pay once and you're done paying. Your heirs are done paying. It's a powerful tool. Here's a simple example to show you how powerful it can be:

Imagine that you pay to convert a traditional IRA to a Roth. You have decided that you want to put the money in a vehicle that gives you a tax-advantaged income option down the road. If you pay a 25 percent tax on that conversion and the Roth IRA then doubles in value over the next 10 years, you could look at your situation as only having paid 12.5 percent tax.

The prospect of tax-advantaged income is a tempting one. While you have to pay a conversion tax to transfer your assets, you also have turned taxable income into tax free retirement money that you can let grow as long as you want without being required to withdraw it.

There are options, however, that address this problem. Much like the Brandeis story, there may be a "free bridge" option for many investors.

Your financial professional will likely tell you that it is not a matter of whether or not you should perform a Roth IRA conversion, it is a matter of how much you should convert and when.

Here are some of the things to consider before converting to a Roth IRA:

- If you make a conversion before you retire, you may end up paying higher taxes on the conversion because it is likely that you are in some of your highest earning years, placing you in the highest tax bracket of your life. It is possible that a better strategy would be to wait until after you retire, a time when you may have less taxable income, which would place you in a lower tax bracket.
- Many people opt to reduce their work hours from fulltime to part-time in the years before they retire. If you have pursued this option, your income will likely be lower, in turn lowering your tax rate.
- The first years that you draw Social Security benefits can also be years of lower reported income, making it another good time frame in which to convert to a Roth IRA.

One key strategy to handling a Roth IRA conversion is to ***always be able to pay the cost of the tax conversion with outside money***. Structuring your tax year to include something like a significant deduction can help you offset the conversion tax. This way you aren't forced to take the money you need for taxes from the value of the IRA. The reason taxes apply to this maneuver is because when you withdraw money from a traditional IRA, it is treated as taxable income by the IRS. Your financial professional, with the help of the CPAs at their firm, may be able to provide you with options like after-tax money, itemized deductions or other situations that can pose effective tax avoidance options.

Some examples of avoiding Roth IRA conversions taxes include:

- *Using medical expenses that are above 10 percent of your Adjusted Gross Income.* If you have health care costs that you can list as itemized deductions, you can convert an amount of income from a traditional IRA to a Roth IRA that is offset by the deductible amount. Essentially, deductible medical expenses negate the taxes resulting from recording the conversion.

- *Individuals, usually small business owners, who are dealing with a Net Operating Loss (NOL).* If you have NOLs, but aren't able to utilize all of them on your tax return, you can carry them forward to offset the taxable income from the taxes on income you convert to a Roth IRA.

- *Charitable giving.* If you are charitably inclined, you can use the amount of your donations to reduce the amount of taxable income you have during that year. By matching the amount you convert to a Roth IRA to the amount your taxable income was reduced by charitable giving, you can essentially avoid taxation on the conversion. You may decide to double your donations to a charity in one year, giving them two years' worth of donations in order to offset the Roth IRA conversion tax on this year's tax return.

- *Investments that are subject to depletion.* Certain investments can kick off depletion expenses. If you make an investment and are subject to depletion expenses, they can be deducted and used to offset a Roth IRA conversion tax.

Not all of the above scenarios work for everyone, and there are many other options for offsetting conversion taxes. The point is that you have options, and your financial professional and tax professional can help you understand those options.

If you have a traditional IRA, Roth conversions are something you should look at. As you approach retirement you should consider your options and make choices that keep more of your money in your pocket, not the government's.

ADDITIONAL TAX BENEFITS OF ROTH IRAS

Not only do Roth IRAs provide you with tax-advantaged growth, they also give you a tax diversified landscape that allows you to maximize your distributions. Chances are that no matter the circumstances, you will have taxed income and other assets subject to taxation. *But if you have a Roth IRA, you have the unique ability to manage your Adjusted Gross Income (AGI), because you have a tax-advantaged income option!*

Converting to a Roth IRA can also help you preserve and build your legacy. Because Roth IRAs are exempt from RMDs, after you make a conversion from a traditional IRA, your Roth account can grow tax-advantaged for another 15, 20 or 25 years and it can be used as tax-advantaged income by your heirs. It is important to note, however, that non-spousal beneficiaries do have to take RMDs from a Roth IRA, or choose to stretch it and draw tax-advantaged income out of it over their lifetime.

TO CONVERT OR NOT TO CONVERT?

Conversions aren't only for retirees. You can convert at any time. Your choice should be based on your individual circumstances and tax situation. Sticking with a traditional IRA or converting to a Roth, again, depends on your individual circumstances, including your income, your tax bracket and the amount of deductions you have each year.

Is it better to have a Roth IRA or traditional IRA? It depends on your individual circumstance. Some people don't mind having taxable income from an IRA. Their income might not be very high and their RMD might not bump their tax bracket up, so it's not as big a deal. A similar situation might involve income from Social Security. Social Security benefits are taxed based on other income you are drawing. If you are in a position where none or very little of your Social Security benefit is subject to taxes, paying income tax on your RMD may be very easy.

» *There are also situations where leveraging taxable income from a traditional IRA can work to your advantage come tax time. For example, Charles and Lucy dream of buying a boat when they retire. It is something they have looked forward to their entire marriage. In addition to the savings and investments that they created to supply them with income during retirement, which includes a traditional IRA, they have also saved money for the sole purpose of purchasing a boat once they stop working.*

When the time comes and they finally buy the boat of their dreams, they pay an additional $15,000 in sales taxes that year because of the large purchase. Because they are retired and earning less money, the deductions they used to be able to realize from their income taxes are no longer there. The high amount of sales taxes they paid on the boat puts them in a position where they could benefit from taking taxable income from a traditional IRA.

When Charles and Lucy's financial professional learns about their purchase, he immediately contacts a CPA at his firm to run the numbers. They determine that by taking a

$15,000 distribution from their IRA, they could fulfill their income needs to offset the $15,000 sales tax deduction that they were claiming due to the purchase of their boat. In the end, they pay zero taxes on their income distribution from their IRA.

The moral of the story? **Having a tax diversified landscape gives you options.** Having capital assets that can be liquidated, tax-advantaged income options and sources that can create capital gains or capital losses will put you in a position to play your cards right no matter what you want to accomplish with your taxes. The ace up your sleeve is your financial professional and the CPAs they work with. Do yourself a favor and *plan* your taxes instead of *reporting* them!

CHAPTER 10 RECAP //
- Look for the "free bridge" option in your tax strategy.
- Converting from a traditional to a Roth IRA can provide you with tax-advantaged retirement income.
- Converting to a Roth IRA can also help you preserve and build your legacy.
- There are many ways to reduce your taxes. Being smart about your Roth IRA conversion is one of the main ways to do so.

11

YOUR LEGACY BEYOND DOLLARS AND CENTS

If you're like most people, planning your estate isn't on the top of your list of things to do. Planning your income needs for retirement, managing your assets and just living your life without worrying about how your estate will be handled when you are gone make legacy planning less than attractive for a Saturday afternoon task. The fact of the matter, however, is that if you don't plan your legacy, someone else will. That someone else is usually a combination of the IRS and other government entities: lawyers, executors, courts, and accountants. Who do you think has the best interests of your beneficiaries in mind?

Today, there is more consideration given to planning a legacy than just maximizing your estate. When most people think about an estate, it may seem like something only the very wealthy have: a stately manor or an enormous business. But a legacy is something else entirely. A legacy is more than the sum total of the financial assets you have accumulated. It is the lasting impression you make on those you leave behind. The dollar and cents are just a small part of a legacy.

A legacy encompasses the stories that others tell about you, shared experiences and values. An estate may pay for college tuition, but a legacy may inform your grandchildren about the importance of higher education and self-reliance.

A legacy may also contain family heirlooms or items of emotional significance. It may be a piece of art your great-grandmother painted, family photos, or a childhood keepsake.

When you go about planning your legacy, certainly explore strategies that can maximize the financial benefit to the ones you care about. But also take the time to ensure that you have organized the whole of your legacy, and let that be a part of the last gift you leave.

Many people avoid planning their legacy until they feel they must. Something may change in your life, like the birth of a grandchild, the diagnosis of a serious health problem, or the death of a close friend or loved one. Waiting for tragedy to strike in order to get your affairs in order is not the best course of action. The emotional stress of that kind of situation can make it hard to make patient, thoughtful decisions. Taking the time to create a premeditated and thoughtful legacy plan will assure that your assets will be transferred where and when you want them when the time comes.

THE BENEFITS OF PLANNING YOUR LEGACY

The distribution of your assets, whether in the form of property, stocks, Individual Retirement Accounts, 401(k)s or liquid assets, can be a complicated undertaking if you haven't left clear instructions about how you want them handled. Not having a plan will cost more money and take more time, leaving your loved ones to wait (sometimes for years) and receive less of your legacy than if you had a clear plan.

Planning your legacy will help your assets be transferred with little delay and little confusion. Instead of leaving decisions about how to distribute your estate to your family, attorneys or financial professionals, preserve your legacy and your wishes by drafting a clear plan at an early age.

And while you know all that, it can still be hard to sit down and do it. It reminds you that life is short, and the relatively complicated nature of sorting through your assets can feel like a daunting task. But one thing is for sure: *it is impossible for your assets to be transferred or distributed the way you want at the end of your life if you don't have a plan.*

Ask yourself:

- Are my assets up to date?
- Have my primary and contingent beneficiaries been clearly designated?
- Does my plan allow for restriction of a beneficiary?
- Does my legacy plan address minor children that I want to provide with income?
- Does my legacy plan allow for multi-generational payout?

Answers to these questions are critical if you want the final say in how your assets are distributed. In order to achieve your legacy goals, you need a plan.

MAKING A PLAN

Eventually, when your income need is filled and you have sufficient standby money to meet your need for emergencies, travel or other extra expenses you are planning for, whatever isn't used during your lifetime becomes your financial legacy. The money that you do not use during your lifetime will either go to loved ones, unloved ones, charity, or the IRS. The question is, who would you rather disinherit?

By having a legacy plan that clearly outlines your assets, your beneficiaries and your distribution goals, you can make sure that your money and property is ending up in the hands of the people you determine beforehand. Is it really that big of a deal? It absolutely is. Think about it. Without a clear plan, it is impossible for anyone to know if your beneficiary designations are current and reflect your wishes because you haven't clearly expressed who your beneficiaries are. You may have an idea of who you want your assets to go to, but without a plan, it is anyone's guess. It is also impossible to know if the titling of your assets is accurate unless you have gone through and determined whose name is on the titles. More importantly, *if you have not clearly and effectively communicated your desires regarding the planned distribution of your legacy, you and your family may end up losing a large part of it.*

As you can see, managing a legacy is more complicated than having an attorney read your will, divide your estate and write checks to your heirs. The additional issue of taxes, Family Maximum Benefit calculations and a host of other decisions rear their heads. Educating yourself about the best options for positioning your legacy assets is a challenging undertaking. Working with a financial professional who is versed in determining the most efficient and effective ways of preserving and distributing your legacy can save you time, money and strife.

So, how do you begin?

Making a Legacy Plan Starts with a Simple List. The first, and one of the largest, steps to setting up an estate plan with a financial professional that reflects your desires is creating a detailed inventory of your assets and debts (if you have any). You need to know what assets you have, who the beneficiaries are, how much they are worth and how they are titled. You can start by identifying and listing your assets. This is a good starting point for working with a financial professional who can then help you determine the detailed information about your assets that will dictate how they are distributed upon your death.

If you are particularly concerned about leaving your kids and grandkids a lifetime of income with minimal taxes, you will want to discuss a Stretch IRA option with your financial professional.

STRETCH IRAS: GETTING THE MOST OUT OF YOUR MONEY

In 1986, the U.S. Congress passed a law that allows for multigenerational distributions of IRA assets. This type of distribution is called a Stretch IRA because it stretches the distribution of the account out over a longer period of time to several beneficiaries. It also allows the account to continue accumulating value throughout your relatives' lifetimes. You can use a Stretch IRA as an income tool that distributes throughout your lifetime, your children's lifetimes and your grandchildren's lifetimes.

Stretch IRAs are an attractive option for those more concerned with creating income for their loved ones than leaving them with a lump sum that may be subject to a high tax rate. With traditional IRA distributions, non-spousal beneficiaries must generally take distributions from their inherited IRAs, whether transferred or not, within five years after the death of the IRA owner. An exception to this rule applies if the beneficiary elects to take distributions over his or her lifetime, which is referred to as stretching the IRA.

Let's begin by looking at the potential of stretching an IRA throughout multiple generations.

» *In this scenario, Mr. Cleaver has an IRA with a current balance of $350,000. If we assume a five percent annual rate of return, and a 28 percent tax rate, the Stretch IRA turned*

Beneficiaries Stretch IRA Distributions

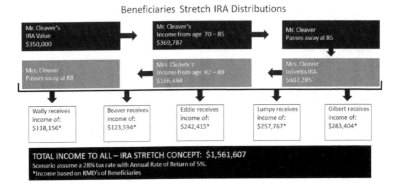

| Mr. Cleaver's IRA Value $350,000 | → | Mr. Cleaver's Income from age 70 – 85 $369,787 | → | Mr. Cleaver Passes away at 85 |

| Mrs. Cleaver Passes away at 88 | ← | Mrs. Cleaver's Income from age 82 – 88 $166,484 | ← | Mrs. Cleaver Inherits IRA $607,285 |

| Wally receives income of: $118,156* | Beaver receives income of: $123,594* | Eddie receives income of: $242,415* | Lumpy receives income of: $257,767* | Gilbert receives income of: $283,404* |

TOTAL INCOME TO ALL – IRA STRETCH CONCEPT: $1,561,607
Scenario assume a 28% tax rate with Annual Rate of Return of 5%.
*Income based on RMD's of Beneficiaries

Beneficiaries FAIL to Stretch IRA Distributions

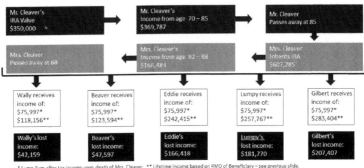

| Mr. Cleaver's IRA Value $350,000 | → | Mr. Cleaver's Income from age 70 – 85 $369,787 | → | Mr. Cleaver Passes away at 85 |

| Mrs. Cleaver Passes away at 88 | ← | Mrs. Cleaver's Income from age 82 – 88 $166,484 | ← | Mrs. Cleaver Inherits IRA $607,285 |

| Wally receives income of: $75,997* $118,156** | Beaver receives income of: $75,997* $123,594** | Eddie receives income of: $75,997* $242,415** | Lumpy receives income of: $75,997* $257,767** | Gilbert receives income of: $75,997* $283,404** |

| Wally's lost income: $42,159 | Beaver's lost income: $47,597 | Eddie's lost income: $166,418 | Lumpy's lost income: $181,770 | Gilbert's lost income: $207,407 |

* Lump Sum after tax income upon death of Mrs. Cleaver. ** Lifetime income based on RMD of Beneficiary – see previous slide.

a $502,625 legacy into more than $1.5 million. Doubling the value of the IRA also provided Mr. Cleaver, his wife, two children and three grandchildren with income. Not choosing the stretch option would have cost nearly $800,000 and had impacts on six of Mr. Cleaver's loved ones.

Unfortunately, many things may also play a role in failing to stretch IRA distributions. It can be tempting for a beneficiary to take a lump sum of money despite the tax consequences. Fortunately, if you want to solidify your plan for distribution, there are

YOUR LEGACY BEYOND DOLLARS AND CENTS

options that will allow you to open up an IRA and incorporate "spendthrift" clauses for your beneficiaries. This will ensure your legacy is stretched appropriately and to your specifications. Only certain insurance companies allow this option, and you will not find this benefit with any brokerage accounts. You need to work with a financial professional who has the appropriate relationship with an insurance company that provides this option.

CHAPTER 11 RECAP //

- Your legacy encompasses more than just the physical assets left behind for your children, grandchildren and charities or organizations. It's how you will be remembered.
- Managing a legacy is more complicated than having an attorney read your will, divide your estate, and write checks to your heirs. Issues such as taxes, Family Maximum Benefit calculations and a host of other concerns make it necessary to educate yourself. Working with a financial professional can save you time, money and stress.
- Legacy planning begins with a simple list.

12
PREPARING YOUR LEGACY

Being a planner, Sam Weston organized his assets long ago. He and Louise started planning their retirement early and made investment decisions that would meet their needs. With a combination of IRA to Roth IRA conversions, a series of income annuities and a well-planned money management strategy overseen by his financial professional, he easily filled his income gap and was able to focus on ways to accumulate his wealth throughout his retirement. He reorganized his Red Money and Green Money as he got older. When Sam retired, he had an income plan created that allowed him to maximize his Social Security benefit. He even had enough to accumulate wealth during his retirement. At this point, Sam turned his attention to planning his legacy. He wanted to know how he could maximize the amount of his legacy he will pass on to his grandchildren.

Sam met with an attorney to draw up a will, but he quickly learned that while having a will was a good plan, it wasn't the most efficient way to distribute his legacy. In fact, relying solely on a will created several roadblocks.

The two main problems that arose for Sam were *Probate* and *Unintentional Disinheritance:*

Problem #1: Probate

Probate. Just speaking the word out loud can cause shivers to run down your spine. Probate's ugly reputation is well deserved. It can be a costly, time consuming process that diminishes your estate and can delay the distribution of your estate to your loved ones. Nasty stuff, by any measure. Unless you have made a clear legacy plan and discussed options for avoiding probate, it is highly likely that you have many assets that might pass through probate needlessly. ***If your will and beneficiary designations aren't correctly structured, some of these assets will go through the probate process, which can turn dollars into cents.***

If you have a will, probate is usually just a formality. There is little risk that your will won't be executed per your instructions. The problem arises when the costs and lengthy timeline that probate creates come into play. Probate proceedings are notoriously expensive, lengthy and ponderous. A typical probate process identifies all of your assets and debts, pays any taxes and fees that you owe (including estate tax), pays court fees, and distributes your property and assets to your heirs. This process usually takes at least a year, and can take even longer before your heirs actually receive anything that you have left for them. For this reason, and because of the sometimes exorbitant fees that may be charged by lawyers and accountants during the process, probate has earned a nasty reputation.

Probate can also be a painstakingly public process. Because the probate process happens in court, the assets you own that go through a probate procedure become part of the public record.

While this may not seem like a big deal to some, other people don't want that kind of intimate information available to the public.

Additionally, if your estate is entirely distributed via your will, there is a risk that the money that your family may need to cover the costs of your medical bills, funeral expenses and estate taxes could be tied up in probate, which can last up to a year or more. While immediate family members may have the option of requesting immediate cash from your assets during probate to cover immediate health care expenses, taxes, and fees, that process comes with its own set of complications. Choosing alternative methods for distributing your legacy can make life easier for your loved ones and can help them claim more of your estate in a more timely fashion than traditional methods.

A simpler and less tedious approach is to avoid probate altogether by structuring your estate to be distributed outside of the probate process. Two common ways of doing this are by structuring your assets inside a life insurance plan, and by using individual retirement planning tools like IRAs that give you the option of designating a beneficiary upon your death.

Problem #2: Unintentionally Disinheriting Your Family

You would never want to unintentionally disinherit a loved one or loved ones because of confusion surrounding your legacy plan. Unfortunately, it happens. Why? This terrible situation is typically caused by a simple lack of understanding. In particular, mistakes regarding legacy distribution occur with regards to those whom people care for the most: their grandchildren.

One of the most important ways to plan for the inheritance of your grandchildren is by properly structuring the distribution of your legacy. Specifically, you need to know if your legacy is going to be distributed *per stirpes* or *per capita*.

Per Stirpes. *Per stirpes* is a legal term in Latin that means "by the branch." Your estate will be distributed *per stirpes* if you designate each branch of your family to receive an equal share of your estate. In the event that your children predecease you, their share will be distributed evenly between their children — your grandchildren.

Per Capita. *Per capita* distribution is different in that you may designate different amounts of your estate to be distributed to members of the same generation.

Per stirpes distribution of assets will follow the family tree down the line as the predecessor beneficiaries pass away. On the other hand, per capita distribution of assets ends on the branch of the family tree with the death of a designated beneficiary. For example, when your child passes away, in a per capita distribution, your grandchildren would not receive distributions from the assets that you designated to your child.

What the terms mean is not nearly as important as what they do, however. The reality is that improperly titled assets could accidentally leave your grandchildren disinherited upon the death of their parents. It's easy to check, and it's even easier to fix.

A simple way to remember the difference between the two types of distribution goes something like this: "***Stirpes are forever and Capita is capped.***"

Another way to avoid complicated legacy distribution problems, and the probate process, is by leveraging a life insurance plan.

LIFE INSURANCE: AN IMPORTANT LEGACY TOOL

One of the most powerful legacy tools you can leverage is a good life insurance policy. Life insurance is a highly efficient legacy tool because it creates money when it is needed or desired the most. Over the years, life insurance has become less expensive, while it offers more features, and it provides longer guarantees.

There are many unique benefits of life insurance that can help your beneficiaries get the most out of your legacy. Some of them include:

- Providing beneficiaries with a tax-free, liquid asset.
- Covering the costs associated with your death.
- Providing income for your dependents.
- Offering an investment opportunity for your beneficiaries.
- Covering expenses such as tuition or mortgage down payments for your children or grandchildren.

Very few people want life insurance, but nearly everyone wants what it does. Life insurance is specifically, and uniquely, capable of creating money when it is needed most. When a loved one passes, no amount of money can remove the pain of loss. And certainly, money doesn't solve the challenges that might arise with losing someone important.

It has been said that when you have money, you have options. When you don't have money, your options are severely limited. You might imagine a life insurance policy can give your family and loved ones options that would otherwise be impossible.

» *Nathan spent the last 20 years building a small business. In so many ways, it is a family business. Each of his three children, Katelynn, Emma and Sam, worked in the shop part-time during high school, and his wife, Emily, helped with the books. But after all three kids attended college and moved on to start their lives, only Emma returned to join her father. When Emily's illness progressed and she became wheelchair-bound, it was Emma who stayed near to be with her during her last years. After Nathan's wife passed away, it hit him that Emma would be the one to run the business full-time.*

Nathan is able to retire comfortably on Social Security and on-going income from the shop, but the business represents to him his legacy. While he and his wife set up an account years ago to provide college money for their children, it is his wish that Emma own the business outright. To be fair, however, he also wants to leave an equal legacy to each of his other two children.

There is no simple way to divide the business into thirds and still leave the business intact for Emma.

Nathan ends up buying a life insurance policy to make up the difference. Katelynn and Sam will receive their share of an inheritance in cash from the life insurance policy and Emma will be able to inherit the business intact.

Nathan is able to accomplish all of his goals, treat all three children equitably and leave Emma the business she helped to build.

If you have a life insurance policy but you haven't looked at it in a while, you may not know how it operates, how much it is worth and how it will be distributed to your beneficiaries. You may also need to update your beneficiaries on your policy. In short, without a comprehensive review of your policy, you don't really know where the money will go or to whom it will go.

If you don't have a life insurance policy but are looking for options to maintain and grow your legacy, speaking with a professional can show you the benefits of life insurance. Many people don't consider buying a life insurance policy until some event in their life triggers it, like the loss of a loved one, an accident or a health condition.

BENEFITS OF LIFE INSURANCE

Life insurance is a useful and secure tool for contingency planning, ensuring that your dependents receive the assets that you want them to have, and for meeting the financial goals you have set for the future. While it bears the name "Life Insurance," it is, in reality, a diverse financial tool that can meet many needs. The main function of a life insurance policy is to provide financial assets for your survivors. Life insurance is particularly efficient at achieving this goal because it provides a tax-advantaged lump sum of money in the form of a death benefit to your beneficiary or beneficiaries. That financial asset can be used in a number of ways. It can be structured as an investment to provide income for your spouse or children, it can pay down debts, and it can be used to cover estate taxes and other costs associated with death.

Living Benefits:

As discussed in Chapter Two, Taking Control of Your Assets, many of today's life insurance policies and annuity products also have riders and provisions for increased income in the event of chronic illness. Often known as Living Benefits, these products provide you with the means to pay for home health care or a nursing home facility while you are still alive. With annuities, these benefits are sometimes known as "income doublers" because the fixed income contracted by the rider will double should you or your spouse require long term care. Long term care can include basic custodial services such as cleaning and taking out the garbage, or it can be more involved and include intrinsic nursing services. Even if it's too late to qualify for traditional long term care insurance, long term care riders on annuity and life insurance products might still be an option for you, and if you never need long term care, that money is not lost. Instead, your beneficiaries receive a legacy.

Tax Benefits:

Tax liabilities on the estate you leave behind are inevitable. Capital property, for instance, is taxed at its fair market value at the time of your death, unless that property is transferred to your spouse. If the property has appreciated during the time you owned it, taxation on capital gains will occur. Registered Retirement Savings Plans (RRSPs) and other similarly structured assets are also included as taxable income unless transferred to a beneficiary as well. Those are just a few examples of how an estate can become subject to a heavy tax burden. The unique benefits of a life insurance policy provide ways to handle this tax burden, solving any liquidity problems that may arise if your family members want to hold onto an illiquid asset, such as a piece of property or an investment. Life insurance can provide a significant amount of money to a family member or other beneficiary, and that money is likely to remain exempt from taxation or seizure.

Protection Benefits:
One of life insurance's most important benefits is that it is not considered part of the estate of the policy holder. The death benefit that is paid by the insurance company goes exclusively to the beneficiaries listed on the policy. This shields the proceeds of the policy from fees and costs that can reduce an estate, including probate proceedings, attorneys' fees and claims made by creditors. The distribution of your life insurance policy is also unaffected by delays of the estate's distribution, like probate. Your beneficiaries will get the proceeds of the policy in a timely fashion, regardless of how long it takes for the rest of your estate to be settled.

Investing a portion of your assets in a life insurance policy can also protect that portion of your estate from creditors. If you owe money to someone or some entity at the time of your death, a creditor is not able to claim any money from a life insurance policy or an annuity, for that matter. An exception to this rule would be if you had already used the life insurance policy as collateral against a loan. If a large portion of the money you want to dedicate to your legacy is sitting in a savings account, investment or other liquid form, creditors may be able to receive their claim on it before your beneficiaries get anything, that is if there's anything left. A life insurance policy protects your assets from creditors and ensures that your beneficiaries get the money that you intend them to have.

HOW MUCH LIFE INSURANCE DO YOU NEED?

Determining the type of policy and the amount right for you depends on an analysis of your needs. A financial professional can help you complete a needs analysis that will highlight the amount of insurance that you require to meet your goals. This type of personalized review will allow you to determine ways to continue providing income for your spouse or any dependents you may have. A financial professional can also help you calculate the amount of income that your policy should replace to meet the needs of your beneficiaries and the duration of the distribution of that income.

You may also want to use your life insurance policy to meet any expenses associated with your death. These can include funeral costs, fees from probate and legal proceedings, and taxes. You may also want to dedicate a portion of your policy proceeds to help fund tuition or other expenses for your children or grandchildren. You can buy a policy and hope it covers all of those costs, or you can work with a professional who can calculate exactly how much insurance you need and how to structure it to meet your goals. Which would you rather do?

AVOIDING POTENTIAL SNAGS

There are benefits to having life insurance supersede the direction given in a will or other estate plan, but there are also some potential snags that you should address to meet your wishes. For example, if your will instructs that your assets be divided equally between your two children but your life insurance beneficiary is listed as just one of the children, the assets in the life insurance policy will only be distributed to the child listed as the beneficiary. The beneficiary designation on your life insurance policy supersedes your will's instruction. This is important to understand when designating beneficiaries on a policy you purchase. Work with a professional to make sure that your beneficiaries are accurately listed on your assets, especially your life insurance policies.

USING LIFE INSURANCE TO BUILD YOUR LEGACY

Depending on your goals, there are strategies you can use that could multiply how much you leave behind. Life insurance is one of the most surefire and efficient investment tools for building a substantial legacy that will meet your financial goals.

Here is a brief overview of how life insurance can boost your legacy:

- Life insurance provides an immediate increase in your legacy.
- It provides an income tax-advantaged death benefit for your beneficiaries.
- A good life insurance policy has the opportunity to accumulate value over time.
- It may have an option to include long-term care (LTC) or chronic illness benefits should you require them.

If your Green Money income needs for retirement are met, you may have extra assets that you want to earmark as legacy funds. By electing to invest those assets into a life insurance policy, you can immediately increase the amount of your legacy. Remember, **life insurance allows you to transfer a tax-advantaged lump sum of money to your beneficiaries. It remains in your control during your lifetime, can provide for your long-term care needs and bypasses probate costs.** And make no mistake, taxes can have a huge impact on your legacy. Not only that, income and assets from your legacy can have tax implications for your beneficiaries, as well.

Here's a brief overview of how taxes could affect your legacy and your beneficiaries:

- The higher your income, the higher the rate at which it is taxed.
- Withdrawals from qualified plans are taxed as income.
- What's more, when you leave a large qualified plan, it ends up being taxed at a high rate.
- If you left a $500,000 IRA to your child, they could end up owing as much as $140,000 in income taxes.
- However, if you could just withdraw $50,000 a year, the tax bill might only be $10,000 per year.

How could you use that annual amount to leave a larger legacy? Luckily, you can leverage a life insurance policy to avoid those tax penalties, preserving a larger amount of your legacy and freeing your beneficiaries from an added tax burden.

» *When Darlene turned 70 years old, she decided it was time to look into life insurance policy options. She still feels young, but she remembers that her first husband died early and she wants to plan ahead so she can pass on some of her legacy to her step-children. They have become a close family and Darlene was never able to have children of her own. She wants to be remembered when she goes.*

Darlene doesn't really want to think about life insurance, but she does want the security, reliability and tax-advantaged distribution that it offers. She lives modestly with her new husband, Paul. Their combined Social Security benefits and his income producing assets meet all their income needs. As the beneficiary of her late husband's life insurance policy, she has $100,000 in an account that she does not want to *spend down, and she doesn't anticipate ever needing since her income needs are currently met.*

*After looking at several different investment options with a professional, Darlene decides that a Single Premium life insurance policy fits her needs best. She can buy the policy with a $100,000 one-time payment and she is guaranteed that it would provide more than the value of the contract to her beneficiaries. If she left the money in the CD, it would be subject to taxes. But for every dollar that she puts into the life insurance policy, her beneficiaries are guaranteed at least that dollar plus a death benefit, and all of it will be **tax-free!***

For $100,000, Darlene's particular policy offers a $170,000 death benefit distribution to her beneficiaries. By moving the $100,000 from a CD to a life insurance policy, Darlene increases her legacy by 70 percent. Not only that, she has also sheltered it from taxes, so her beneficiaries will be able to receive $1.70 for every $1.00 that she entered into the policy! While buying the policy doesn't allow her to use the money for herself, it does allow her family to benefit from her well-planned legacy.

MAKE YOUR WISHES KNOWN

Estate taxes used to be a much hotter topic in the mid-2000s when the estate tax limits and exclusions were much smaller and taxed at a higher rate than today. In 2008, estates valued at $2 million or more were taxed at 45 percent. Just two years later, the limit was raised to $5 million dollars taxed at 35 percent. The limit has continued to rise ever since. The limit applies to fewer people than before. Estate organization, however, is just as important as ever, and it affects everyone.

Ask yourself:

- Are your assets actually titled and held the way you think they are?

- Are your beneficiaries set up the way you think they should be?
- Have there been changes to your family or those you desire as beneficiaries?

There is more to your legacy beyond your property, money, investments and other assets that you leave to family members, loved ones and charities. Everyone has a legacy beyond money. You also leave behind personal items of importance, your values and beliefs, your personal and family history, and your wishes. Beyond a will and a plan for your assets, it is important that you make your wishes known to someone for the rest of your personal legacy. When it comes time for your family and loved ones to make decisions after you are gone, knowing your wishes can help them make decisions that honor you and your legacy, and give meaning to what you leave behind. Your professional can help you organize.

Think about your:
- Personal stories / recollections
- Values
- Personal items of emotional significance
- Financial assets

Do you want to make a plan to pass these things on to your family?

WORKING WITH A PROFESSIONAL

Part of using life insurance to your greatest advantage is selecting the policy and provider that can best meet your goals. Venturing into the jungle of policies, brokers and salespeople can be overwhelming, and can leave you wondering if you've made the best decision. Working with a trusted financial professional can help you cut through the red tape, the "sales-speak" and confusion to find a policy that meets your goals and best serves your desires for your money. If you already have a policy, a financial professional can help you review it and become familiar with the policy's premium, the guarantees the policy affords, its performance, and its features and benefits. A financial professional can also help you make any necessary changes to the policy.

> » *When Gloria turned 88, her neighbor, Louise Weston, finally convinced her to meet with a financial professional to help her organize her assets and get her legacy in order. Although Gloria is reluctant to let a stranger in on her personal finances, she ends up very glad that she did.*
>
> *In the process of listing Gloria's assets and her beneficiaries, her professional finds a man's name listed as the beneficiary of an old life insurance annuity that she owns. It turns out, the man is Gloria's ex-husband who is still alive. Had Gloria passed away before her ex-husband, the annuities and any death benefits that came with them, would have been passed on to her ex-husband. This does not reflect her latest wishes.*

Things change, relationships evolve and the way you would like your legacy organized needs to adapt to the changes that happen throughout your life. There may be a new child or grandchild in your family, or you may have been divorced or remarried. A professional will regularly review your legacy assets and ask you questions to make sure that everything is up to date and that the current organization reflects your current wishes.

CHAPTER 12 RECAP //

- Legacy planning tools include the creation of wills, trusts, living wills, and durable power of attorney for health care considerations. An estate planning attorney can help you with your individual needs.

- Review your current life insurance policies in order to determine if refinancing your life insurance makes sense.

- Life insurance provides for the distribution of tax-free, liquid assets to your beneficiaries and can significantly build your legacy. They can also provide Living Benefits to help you pay for the high costs of medical care while you are still living.

- Working with a financial professional can help you select the policy that best meets your needs, or can help you fine -tune your existing policy to better reflect your desires and intentions.

13

CHOOSING A FINANCIAL PROFESSIONAL

How do you find a financial professional you can trust?

Remember George and Dee Weston from Chapter 1? Even though they had Social Security benefits coming, and they had money saved in their 401(k) employee plans, they didn't have a guaranteed source of income. Each year, they were withdrawing principal and watching their savings dwindle away.

Before they met with a financial professional, George and Dee had no plan. They had no idea if their savings would be able to last as long as they did, and they were worried about what the final years of their retirement would look like.

After their meeting, they began to think about their savings in terms of its ability to produce income. They identified the risks their investments were exposed to, and they discussed other risks such as spousal continuation and the rising cost of long term care. Looking at their savings this way clarified what they wanted their money to do. They secured their principal first so it was guaranteed not to diminish. They put that money into multiple investment vehicles that could provide a steady stream of income so they could pay their bills every month from the moment they retired until the day they died. They maximized their Social Security benefit by targeting the year and month they would get the most lifetime benefits. Their professional also helped them make decisions that impacted their taxes, protecting the value of their assets and allowing them to keep more of their money in order to create their definition of a legacy. But more than their physical assets, it was their example in proper planning that they passed down to their three sons, Nathan, Sam and Ed, who all went on to build retirement dreams of their own.

This isn't a fairy tale scenario. This is an example of how much you stand to gain by meeting with a financial professional who can help you create a planful approach to your retirement. The concept of I Hope So and I Know So didn't just apply to their money, it also applied to George and Dee. They hoped they had saved enough for retirement, but they didn't understand the amount of risk their assets were exposed to, or how those assets should be positioned in order to provide income. Working with a financial professional allowed them to secure their income needs for the rest of their lives and that gave them the peace of mind to enjoy the retirement they deserved.

Now, ask yourself: Is your retirement built on hopes and dreams, or a solid, predictable plan?

From the moment you dip your toes into the retirement planning pool to the point you start swimming laps, working with a professional that you trust can make all the difference in how well your retirement reflects your desires.

It is important to know what you are looking for before taking the plunge. There are many people who would love to handle your money, but not everyone is qualified to handle it in a way that leads to a holistic approach to creating a solid retirement plan. The distinction being made here is that you should look for someone who puts your interests first and actively wants to help you meet your goals and objectives. Oftentimes, the products someone sells you matter less than their dedication to making sure that you have a plan that meets your needs.

Professionals take your whole financial position into consideration. They make plans that adjust your risk exposure, invest in tools that secure your desired income during retirement and create investment strategies that allow you to continue accumulating wealth during your retirement for you to use later or to contribute to your legacy. If you buy stocks with a broker, use a different agent for a life insurance policy and have an unmanaged 401(k) through your employer, working with a financial professional will consolidate the management of your assets so you have one trustworthy person quarterbacking all of the team elements of your portfolio. Financial products and investment tools change, but the concepts that lie behind wise retirement planning are lasting. In the end, a financial professional's approach is designed for those serious about planning for retirement. *Can you say the same thing about the person who advises you about your financial life?*

It's easy to see how choosing a financial professional can be one of the most important decisions you can make in your life. Not only do they provide you with advice, they also manage the personal assets that supply your retirement income and contribute to your legacy. So, how do you find a good one?

HOW TO FIND A FINANCIAL PROFESSIONAL YOU CAN TRUST

Taking care to select a financial professional is one of the best things you can do for yourself and for your future. Your professional has influence and control of your investment decisions, making their role in your life more than just important. Your financial security and the quality of your retirement depend on the decisions, investment strategies and asset structuring that you and your professional create.

Working with a professional is different than calling up a broker when you want to buy or trade some stock. This isn't a decision that you can hand off to anyone else. You need to bring your time and attention to the table when it comes to finding someone with whom you can entrust your financial life. Separating the wheat from the chaff will take some work, but you'll be happy you did it.

While no one can tell you exactly who to choose or how to choose them, the following information can help you narrow the field:

- You can start by asking your friends, family and colleagues for referrals. You will want to pay particular attention to the recommendations that you get from others who are in your similar financial situation and who have similar lifestyle choices. The professional for the CEO of your company may have a different skill-set than the skill-set of the professional befitting your cousin who has 3 kids and a Subaru like you. Do follow-up research on the Internet as well. Look up the people who have been recommended to you on websites like LinkedIn that show the work history, referrals and experience of the candidates that you find most attractive. You will also learn about the firms with or for whom they work. The investment philosophies and reputations of the companies they work for will tell you a lot about how they will handle your money.

- The other side of the coin, however, is that everyone and their brother has a recommendation about how you should manage your money and who should manage it for you. From hot stock tips to "the best money manager in the state," people love to share good information that makes them look like they are in-the-know. Nobody wants to talk about the bad stock purchases they made, the times they lost money and the poor selections they made regarding financial professionals or stock brokers. If you decide to take a friend or family member's recommendation, make sure they have a substantial, long-term experience with the financial professional and that their glowing review isn't just based on a one-time "win."

- You can also use online tools like the search function of the Financial Planning Association (http://www.fpanet.org/) and the National Association of Personal Financial professionals (http://www.napfa.org/). Most of the professionals listed on these sites do not earn commissions from selling financial products, but are instead paid on a fee-only basis for their services. It is important to understand how your professional is being paid. It is generally considered preferable to work with a fee-based professional who will not have conflicts of interests between earning a commission and acting in your best interests.

- Many professionals may also be brokers or dealers who can earn commissions on things like life insurance, certain types of annuities and disability insurance. These professionals have most likely intentionally overlapped their roles so that if their clients choose to purchase insurance or investment products that require a broker or dealer, those clients won't have to find an additional person to work with. Again, understanding the role of your professional will help you make your determination.

NARROWING THE FIELD

1. Decide on the Type of Professional with Whom You Want to Work. There are four basic kinds of financial professionals. Many professionals may play overlapping roles. It is important to know a professional's primary function, how they charge for their services and whether they are obligated to act in your best interest.

Registered representatives, better known as stockbrokers or bank / investment representatives, make their living by earning commissions on insurance products and investment services. Stockbrokers basically sell you things. The products from which they make the highest commission are sometimes the products that they recommend to their clients. If you want to make a simple transaction, such as buying or selling a particular stock, a registered representative can help you. Although registered representatives are licensed professionals, if you want to create a structured and planful approach to positioning your assets for retirement, you might want to consider continuing your search.

The term "planner" is often misused. It can refer to credible professionals that are CPAs, CFPs and ChFCs to your uncle's next door neighbor who claims to have a lead on some undervalued stock about to be "discovered." A wide array of people may claim to be planners because there are no requirements to be a planner. The term financial planner, however, refers to someone who is properly registered as an investment advisor and serves as a fiduciary as described below.

Financial professionals are the diamonds in the rough. These Registered Investment Advisors are compensated on a fee basis. They do, however, often have licensure as stockbrokers or insurance agents, allowing them to earn commissions on certain transactions. More importantly, **financial professionals are financial fiduciaries, meaning they are required to make financial decisions in your best interest and reflecting your risk tolerance.** Investment Advisors are held to high ethical standards and are highly regarded in the financial industry. Financial professionals also often take a more comprehensive approach to asset management. These professionals are trained and credentialed to plan and coordinate their clients' assets in order to meet their goals or retirement and legacy planning. They are not focused on individual stocks, investments or markets. They look at the big picture, the whole enchilada.

Money managers are on par with financial professionals. However, they are often given explicit permission to make investment decisions without advanced approval by their clients.

Understanding the person you are working with and their title is the first step to planning your retirement. While each of the above-mentioned types of financial professionals can help you with aspects of your finances, it is **financial professionals** who have the most intimate role, the most objective investment strategies and the most unbiased mode of compensation for their services. A financial professional can also help you with the non-financial aspects of your legacy and can help you find ways to create a tax planning strategy to help you save money.

2. Be Objective. At the end of the day, you need to separate the weak from the strong. While you might want a strong personal rapport with your professional, or you may want to choose your professional for their personality and positive attitude, it is more important that you find someone who will give sage advice regarding achieving your retirement goals.

It can be helpful to use a process of elimination to narrow the field of potential professionals. Look into five or six potential leads and cross off your list the ones that don't meet your requirements until only one or two remain. Cross-check your remaining choices against the list of things you need from a professional. Make sure they represent a firm that has the investment tools and products that you desire, and make sure they have experience in retirement planning. That is, after all, the main goal.

Don't be afraid to investigate each of your candidates. You'll want to ask the same questions and look for the same information from everyone you consider so you can then compare them and discern which is best for you. You'll want to take a look at the specific credentials of each professional, their experience and competence, their ethics and fiduciary status, their history and track record, and a list of the services that they offer. The professionals who meet all or most of your qualifications are the ones you will contact for an interview.

Potential professionals should meet your qualifications in the following categories:

- *Credentials:* Look at their experience, the quality of their education, any associations to which they belong and certifications they have earned. Someone who has continued their professional education through ongoing certifications will be more up-to-date on current financial practices compared to someone who got their degree 25 years ago and hasn't done a thing since.

- *Practices:* Look at the track record of your candidates, how they are compensated for their services, the reports and analysis they offer, and their value added services.

- *Services:* Your professional must meet your needs. If you are planning your retirement, you should work with someone who offers services that help you to that end. You want someone who can offer planning, advice on investment strategies, ways to calculate risk, advice on insurance and annuities products, and ways to manage your tax strategy.

- *Ethics:* You want to work with someone who is above board and does things the right way. Vet them by checking their compliance record, current licensing, fiduciary status and, yes, even their criminal record. You never know!

3. Ask for and Check References. Once you have selected two or three professionals who you want to meet, call or email them and ask for references. Every professional should be able to provide you with at least two or three names. In fact, they will probably be eager to share them with you. Most professionals rely on references for validation of their success, quality of services and likability. You should, however, take them with a grain of salt. You have no way to know whether or not references are a professional's friends or colleagues.

It is worth contacting references, however, to check for inconsistencies. Ask each reference the same set of questions to get the same basic information. How long have they been working with the professional? What kind of services have they used and were they happy with them? What type of financial planning did they use the professional for? Were they versed in the type of financial planning that you needed? You can also ask them direct questions to elicit candid responses. What was the full cost of the expenses that your professional charged you? Do the reports and statements you receive come from the same firm? Questions like these can help you get a sense of how well the reference knows their professional and whether or not they are a quality reference.

A good reference is a bit like icing on the cake. It's nice to have them, but nothing speaks louder than a good track record and quality experience. And remember that a good reference, while nice to hear, is relatively cheap. How many times have you heard someone on the golf course or at work telling you how great their stockbroker is? But how many times have you heard about the bad investments or losses they have experienced?

4. Use the Internet. As a final step before picking up the phone and calling your candidates, do some digging to discover if anyone on your list has a history of unlawful or unethical practices, or has been disciplined for any of their professional behavior or decisions. Don't worry, you don't have to hire a private investigator. You can easily find this information on the Financial Industry Regulatory Authority's (FINRA) online BrokerCheck tool: http://www.finra.org/Investors/ToolsCalculators/BrokerCheck/.

You should obviously explore the website of a potential professional and the website of the firm that they represent. The Internet allows you to go beyond the online business card of a professional to gain access to information that they don't control. It may all be good information! Or a brief search of the Internet could reveal a sketchy past. The best part is that the Internet allows you to find helpful information in an anonymous fashion.

Start with Google (www.google.com) and search the name of a potential professional and their firm. Keep your eyes trained on third party sources such as articles, blog posts or news stories that mention the professional. You can also check a professional's compliance records online with the Financial Industry Regulatory Authority (FINRA) and the Securities and Exchange Commission (SEC). If you want to dig deeper, you can combine search terms like "scams," "lawsuits," "suspensions" and "fraud" with a professional's or firm's name to see what information arises. More likely than not, you won't find anything. But if you do, you'll be glad that you checked.

HOW TO INTERVIEW CANDIDATES

After vetting your candidates and narrowing down a list of professionals that you think might be a good fit for you, it's time to start interviewing.

When you meet in person with a professional who wants to take advantage of your time with them. The presentations and information that they share with you will be important to pay attention to, but you will also want to control some aspects of the interview. After a professional has told you what they want you to hear, it's time to ask your own questions to get the specific information you need to make your decision.

Make sure to prepare a list of questions and an informal agenda so that you can keep track of what you want to ask and what points you want the professional to touch on during the interview. Using the same questions and agenda will also allow you to more easily compare the professionals after you have interviewed them all. Remember that these interviews are just that, *interviews*. You are meeting with several professionals to determine with whom you want to work. Don't agree to anything or sign anything during an interview until after you have made your final decision.

It can also be helpful to put a time limit on your interviews and to meet the professionals at their offices. The time limit will keep things on track and will allow structured time for presentations and questions/discussion. By meeting them at their office, you can get a sense of the work environment, the staff culture and attitude, and how the firm does business. If you are unable to travel to a professional's office and must meet them at your home or office, make sure that your interviews are scheduled with plenty of time between so the professionals don't cross each other's paths.

You can use the following questions during an initial interview to get an understanding of how each professional does business and whether they are a good fit for you:

1. How do you charge for your services? How much do you charge? This information should be easy to find on their website, but if you don't see it, ask. Find out if they charge an initial planning fee, if they charge a percentage for assets under their management and if they make money by selling specific financial products or services. If so, you should follow up by asking how much the service costs. This will give you an idea of how they really make their money and if they have incentive to sell certain products over others. Make sure you understand exactly how you will be charged so there are no surprises down the road if you decide to work with this person.

2. What are your credentials, licenses, and certifications? There are Certified Financial Planners (CFPs), Chartered Financial Consultants (ChFCs), Investment Advisor Representatives, Certified Public Accountants (CPAs) and Personal Financial Specialists (PFSs). Whatever their credentials or titles, you want to be sure that the professional you work with is an expert in the field relevant to your circumstances. If you want someone to manage your money, you will most likely look for an Investment Advisor. Someone that works with an independent firm will likely have a team of CPAs, CFPs and other financial experts upon whom they can draw. If you like the professional you are meeting with and you think they might be a good fit, but they don't have the accounting experience you want them to have, ask about their firm and the resources available to them. If they work closely with CPAs that are experienced in your needs, it could be a good match.

3. What are the financial services that you and your firm provide? The question within the question here is, "Can you help me achieve my goals?" Some people can only provide you with investment advice, and others are tax consultants. You will likely want to work with someone that provides a complete suite of financial planning services and products that touch on retirement planning, insurance options, legacy and estate structuring, and tax planning. Whatever services they provide, make sure they meet your needs and your anticipated needs.

4. What kinds of clients do you work with the most? A lot of financial professionals work within a niche: retirement planning, risk assessment, life insurance, etc. Finding someone who works with other people who are in the same financial boat as you and who have similar goals can be an important way to make sure they understand your needs. While someone might be a crackerjack annuities cowboy, you might not be interested in that option. Ask follow-up questions that will really help you understand where their expertise lies and whether or not their experience lines up with your needs.

5. May I see a sample of one of your financial plans? You wouldn't buy a car without test driving it, and you should not work with a professional without seeing a sample of how they do business. While there is no formal structure that a financial plan has to follow, the variation between professionals can help you find someone who "speaks your language." One professional may provide you with an in-depth analysis that relies heavily on info graphics and diagrams. Someone else may give you a seven page review of your assets and general recommendations. By seeing a sample plan, you can narrow down who presents information in the way that you desire and in ways that you understand.

6. How do you approach investing? You may be entirely in the dark about how to approach your investments, or you might have some guiding principles. Either way, ask each candidate what their philosophy is. Some will resonate with you and some won't. A good professional who has a realistic approach to investing won't promise you the moon or tell you that they can make you a lot of money. Professionals who are successful at retirement planning and full service financial management will tell you that they will listen to your goals, risk tolerance and comfort level with different types of investment strategies. Working with someone who you trust is critical, and this question in particular can help you find out who you can and who you can't.

7. How do you remain in contact with your clients? Does your prospective professional hold annual, quarterly or monthly meetings? How often do *you* want to meet with your professional? Some people want to check in once a year, go over everything and make sure their ducks are all in a row. If any changes over the previous year or additions to their legacy planning strategy came up, they'll do it on that date. Other people want a monthly update to be more involved in the decision making process and to understand what's happening with their portfolio. You basically need to determine the right degree of involvement for both you and your financial professional. You'll also want to feel out how your professional communicates. Do you prefer phone calls or face-to-face meetings? Do you want your professional to explain things to you in detail or to summarize for you what decisions they've made? Is the professional willing to give you their direct phone number or their email address? More importantly, do you want that information and do you want to be able to contact them in those ways?

8. Are you my main contact, or do you work with a team? This is another way of finding out how involved with you your professional will be, and how often they will meet with you. It is also a way to discover how the firm they represent operates and manages their clients. Some professionals will answer their own phone, meet with you regularly and have your home phone number on speed dial. Others will meet with you once a year and have a partner or assistant check in with you every quarter to give you an update. Other companies take an entirely team-based approach whereby clients have a main contact but their portfolio is handled by a team of professionals that represent the firm. One way isn't better than another, but one way will be best for you. Find out how the professional you are interviewing operates before entering into an agreement.

9. How do you provide a unique experience for your clients? This is a polite way of asking, "Why should I work with you?" A professional should have a compelling answer to this question that connects with you. Their answer will likely touch on their investment philosophy, their communication style and their expertise. If you hear them describing strengths and philosophies that resonate with you, keep them on your list. Some professionals will tell you that they will make investments with your money that match your values, others will say they will maximize your returns and others will say they will protect your capital while structuring your assets for income. Whatever you're looking for in a professional, you will most likely find it in the answer to this question.

This last question you will want to ask *yourself* after you've met with someone who you are considering hiring:

10. Did they ask questions and show signs that they were interested in working with me? A professional who will structure your assets to reflect your risk tolerance and to position you for a comfortable retirement must be a good listener. You will want to pass by a professional who talks non-stop and tells you what to do without listening to what you want them to do. If you felt they listened well and understood your needs, and seemed interested and experienced in your situation, then they might be right for you.

THE IMPORTANCE OF INDEPENDENCE
Not all investment firms and financial professionals are created equal. The information in this book has systematically shown that leveraging investments for income and accumulation in today's market requires new ideas and modern planning. In short, you need innovative ideas to come up with the creative solutions

that will provide you with the retirement that you want. Innovation thrives on independence. No matter how good a financial professional is, the firm that they represent needs to operate on principles that make sense in today's economy. Remember, advice about money has been around forever. Good advice, however, changes with the times.

Timing the market, relying on the sale of stocks for income and banking on high treasury and bond returns are not strategies. They aren't even realistic ways to make money or to generate income. Working with an independent agent can help you break free from the old ways of thinking and position you to create a realistic retirement plan.

Working with an independent professional who relies on fee-based income tied to the success of their performance will also give you greater peace of mind. When you do well, they do well, and that's the way it should be. Your independent financial professional will make sure that:

- Your assets are organized and structured to reflect your risk tolerance.
- Your assets will be available to you when you need them and in the way that you need them.
- You will have a lifetime income that will support your lifestyle through your retirement.
- You are handling your taxes as efficiently as possible.
- Your legacy is in order.
- Your Red Money is turned into Green Money.

IT'S WORTH IT!

Finding, interviewing and selecting a financial professional can seem like a daunting task. And honestly, it will take a good amount of work to narrow the field and find the one you want. In the end, it is worth the blood, sweat and tears. Your retirement, lifestyle, assets and legacy are all on the line. The choices you make today will have lasting impacts on your life and the life of your loved ones. Working with someone you trust and know you can rely on to make decisions that will benefit you is invaluable. The work it takes to find them is something you will never regret.

Here is a recap of why working with a financial professional is the best retirement decision you can make:

CHAPTER 13 RECAP //

- A good financial professional puts your needs first. Your risk tolerance, goals, objectives, needs, wants, liquidity concerns and timeline worries should be the focus of the meeting before they try to sell you any products. A plan is only good if it is a good fit for you and your family.

- Finding a financial professional you can trust is imperative, because money isn't just about numbers; it's about the life events and the people that come attached to those numbers.

- To find a professional you can trust, start by asking family and friends for referrals. Make sure to do your due diligence and check out the references of anyone who is recommended to you. Look for resources online such as the Financial Planning Association and the National Association of Personal Financial professionals.

- When interviewing candidates, make sure you understand how they charge for their services. Also look for credentials, licenses and certifications. Ask questions such as: How often do you check in with your clients? May I see a sample of one of your financial plans? And, How do you approach investing? These questions will help ensure that you and your professional are a good fit for each other.

GLOSSARY*

ANNUAL RESET *(ANNUAL RATCHET, CLIQUET)* – Crediting methods measuring index movement over a one year period. Positive interest is calculated and credited at the end of each contract year and cannot be lost if the index subsequently declines. Say that the index increased from 100 to 110 in one year and the indexed annuity had an 80 percent participation rate. The insurance company would take the 10 percent gross index gain for the year (110-100/100), apply the participation rate (10 percent index gain x 80 percent rate) and credit 8 percent interest to the annuity. But, what if in the following year the index declined back to 100? The individual would keep the 8 percent interest earned and simply

---

*"Glossary of Terms." FixedAnnuityFacts.com. NAFA, the National Association for Fixed Annuities, n.d. 12 Nov. 2013

receive zero interest for the down year. An annual reset structure preserves credited gains and treats negative index periods as years with zero growth.

ANNUITANT – The person, usually the annuity owner, whose life expectancy is used to calculate the income payment amount on the annuity.

ANNUITY – An annuity is a contract issued by an insurance company that often serves as a type of savings plan used by individuals looking for long term growth and protection of assets that will likely be needed within retirement.

AVERAGING – Index values may either be measured from a start point to an end point (point-to-point) or values between the start point and end point may be averaged to determine an ending value. Index values may be averaged over the days, weeks, months or quarters of the period.

BENEFICIARY – A beneficiary is the person designated to receive payments due upon the death of the annuity owner or the annuitant themselves.

BONUS RATE – A bonus rate is the "extra" or "additional" interest paid during the first year (the initial guarantee period), typically used as an added incentive to get consumers to select their annuity policy over another.

CALL OPTION *(ALSO SEE PUT OPTION)* – Gives the holder the right to buy an underlying security or index at a specified price on or before a given date.

CAP – The maximum interest rate that will be credited to the annuity for the year or period. The cap usually refers to the maximum interest credited after applying the participation rate or yield spread. If the index methodology showed a 20 percent increase with a participation rate of 60 percent and a maximum interest cap of 10 percent, the contract would credit 10 percent interest. A few annuities use a maximum gain cap instead of a maximum interest cap with the participation rate or yield spread applied to the lesser of the gain or the cap. If the index methodology showed a 20 percent increase with a participation rate of 60 percent and a maximum interest cap of 10 percent, the contract would credit 6 percent interest.

COMPOUND INTEREST – Interest is earned on both the original principal and on previously earned interest. It is more favorable than simple interest. Suppose that your original principal was $1 and your interest rate was 10 percent for five years. With simple interest, your value is ($1 + $0.10 interest each year) = $1.50. With compound interest, your value is ($1 x 1.10 x 1.10 x 1.10 x 1.10 x 1.10) = $1.61. The advantage of compound interest over simple interest becomes greater as each subsequent period passes.

CREDITING METHOD *(ALSO SEE METHODOLOGY)* – The formula(s) used to determine the excess interest that is credited above the minimum interest guarantee.

DEATH BENEFITS – The payment the annuity owner's estate or beneficiaries will receive if he or she dies before the annuity matures. On most annuities, this is equal to the current account value. Some annuities offer an enhanced value at death via an optional rider that has a monthly or annual fee associated with it.

EXCESS INTEREST – Interest credited to the annuity contract above the minimum guaranteed interest rate. In an indexed annuity the excess interest is determined by applying a stated crediting method to a specific index or indices.

FIXED ANNUITY – A contract issued by an insurance company guaranteeing a minimum interest rate with the crediting of excess interest determined by the performance of the insurer's general account. Index annuities are fixed annuities.

FIXED DEFERRED ANNUITY – With fixed annuities, an insurance company offers a guaranteed interest rate plus safety of your principal and earnings (subject to the claims-paying ability of the insurance company). Your interest rate will be reset periodically, based on economic and other factors, but is guaranteed to never fall below a certain rate.

FREE WITHDRAWALS – Withdrawals that are free of surrender charges.

INDEX – The underlying external benchmark upon which the crediting of excess interest is based, also a measure of the prices of a group of securities.

IRA *(INDIVIDUAL RETIREMENT ACCOUNT)* – An IRA is a tax-advantaged personal savings plan that lets an individual set aside money for retirement. All or part of the participant's contributions may be tax deductible, depending on the type of IRA chosen and the participant's personal financial circumstances. Distributions from many employer-sponsored retirement plans may be eligible to be rolled into an IRA to continue tax-deferred growth until the funds are needed. An annuity can be used as an IRA; that is, IRA funds can be used to purchase an annuity.

IRA ROLLOVER – IRA rollover is the phrase used when an individual who has a balance in an employer-sponsored retirement plan transfers that balance into an IRA. Such an exchange, when properly handled, is a tax-advantaged transaction.

LIQUIDITY – The ease with which an asset is convertible to cash. An asset with high liquidity provides flexibility, in that the owner can easily convert it to cash at any time, but it also tends to decrease profitability.

MARKET RISK – The risk of the market value of an asset fluctuating up or down over time. In a fixed or fixed indexed annuity, the original principal and credited interest are not subject to market risk. Even if the index declines, the annuity owner would receive no less than their original principal back if they decided to cash in the policy at the end of the surrender period. Unlike a security, indexed annuities guarantee the original premium and the premium is backed by, and is as safe as, the insurance company that issued it (subject to the claims-paying ability of the insurance company).

METHODOLOGY *(ALSO SEE CREDITING METHOD)* – The way that interest crediting is calculated. On fixed indexed annuities, there are a variety of different methods used to determine how index movement becomes interest credited.

MINIMUM GUARANTEED RETURN *(MINIMUM INTEREST RATE)* – Fixed indexed annuities typically provide a minimum guaranteed return over the life of the contract. At the time that the owner chooses to terminate the contract, the cash surrender value is compared to a second value calculated using the minimum guaranteed return and the higher of the two values is paid to the annuity owner.

OPTION – A contract which conveys to its holder the right, but not the obligation, to buy or sell something at a specified price on or before a given date. After this given date the option ceases to exist. Insurers typically buy options to provide for the excess interest potential. Options may be American style whereby they may be exercised at any time prior to the given date, or they may have to be exercised only during a specified window. Options that may only be exercised during a specified period are European-style options.

OPTION RISK – Most insurers create the potential for excess interest in an indexed annuity by buying options. Say that you could buy a share of stock for $50. If you bought the stock and it rose to $60 you could sell it and net a $10 profit. But, if the stock price fell to $40 you'd have a $10 loss. Instead of buying the actual stock, we could buy an option that gave us the right to buy the stock for $50 at any time over the next year. The cost of the option is $2. If the stock price rose to $60 we would exercise our option, buy the stock at $50 and make $10 (less the $2 cost of the option). If the price of the stock fell to $40, $30 or $10, we wouldn't use the option and it would expire. The loss is limited to $2 – the cost of the option.

PARTICIPATION RATE – The percentage of positive index movement credited to the annuity. If the index methodology determined that the index increased 10 percent and the indexed annuity participated in 60 percent of the increase, it would be said that the contract has a 60 percent participation rate. Participation rates may also be expressed as asset fees or yield spreads.

POINT-TO-POINT – A crediting method measuring index move-ment from an absolute initial point to the absolute end point for a period. An index had a period starting value of 100 and a period ending value of 120. A point-to-point method would record a positive index movement of 20 [120-100] or a 20 percent positive movement [(120-100)/100]. Point-to-point usually refers to annual periods; however the phrase is also used instead of term end point to refer to multiple year periods.

PREMIUM BONUS – A premium bonus is additional money that is credited to the accumulation account of an annuity policy under certain conditions.

PUT OPTION *(ALSO SEE CALL OPTION)* – Gives the holder the right to sell an underlying security or index at a specified price on or before a given date.

QUALIFIED ANNUITIES *(QUALIFIED MONEY)* – Qualified annuities are annuities purchased for funding an IRA, 403(b) tax-deferred annuity or other type of retirement arrangements. An IRA or qualified retirement plan provides the tax deferral. An annuity contract should be used to fund an IRA or qualified retirement plan to benefit from an annuity's features other than tax deferral, including the safety features, lifetime income payout option and death benefit protection.

REQUIRED MINIMUM DISTRIBUTION *(RMD)* – The amount of money that Traditional, SEP and SIMPLE IRA owners and qualified plan participants must begin distributing from their retirement accounts by April 1 following the year they reach age 70.5. RMD amounts must then be distributed each subsequent year.

RETURN FLOOR – Another way of saying minimum guaranteed return.

ROTH IRA – Like other IRA accounts, the Roth IRA is simply a holding account that manages your stocks, bonds, annuities, mutual funds and CD's. However, future withdrawals (including earnings and interest) are typically tax-advantaged once the account has been open for five years and the account holder is age 59.5.

RULE OF 72 – Tells you approximately how many years it takes a sum to double at a given rate. It's handy to be able to figure out, without using a calculator, that when you're earning a 6 percent return, for example, by dividing 6 percent into 72, you'll find that it takes 12 years for money to double. Conversely, if you know it took a sum twelve years to double you could divide 12 into 72 to determine the annual return (6 percent).

SIMPLE INTEREST *(ALSO SEE COMPOUND INTEREST)* – Interest is only earned on the principal balance.

SPLIT ANNUITY – A split annuity is the term given to an effective strategy that utilizes two or more different annuity products – one designed to generate monthly income and the other to restore the original starting principal over a set period of time.

STANDARD & POOR'S 500 *(S&P 500)* – The most widely used external index by fixed indexed annuities. Its objective is to be a benchmark to measure and report overall U.S. stock market performance. It includes a representative sample of 500 common stocks from companies trading on the New York Stock Exchange, American Stock Exchange, and NASDAQ National Market System. The index represents the price or market value of the underlying stocks and does not include the value of reinvested dividends of the underlying stocks.

STOCK MARKET INDEX – A report created from a type of statistical measurement that shows up or down changes in a specific financial market, usually expressed as points and as a percentage, in a number of related markets, or in an economy as a whole (i.e. S&P 500 or New York Stock Exchange).

SURRENDER CHARGE – A charge imposed for withdrawing funds or terminating an annuity contract prematurely. There is no industry standard for surrender charges, that is, each annuity product has its own unique surrender charge schedule. The charge is usually expressed as a percentage of the amount withdrawn prematurely from the contract. The percentage tends to decline over time, ultimately becoming zero.

TRADITIONAL IRA – See <u>IRA (Individual Retirement Account)</u>

TERM END POINT – Crediting methods measuring index movements over a greater timeframe than a year or two. The opposite of an annual reset method. Also referred to as a term point-to-point method. Say that the index value was at 100 on the first day of the period. If the calculated index value was at 150 at the end of the period the positive index movement would be 50 percent (150-100/100). The company would credit a percentage of this movement as excess interest. Index movement is calculated and interest credited at the end of the term and interim movements during the period are ignored.

TERM HIGH POINT *(HIGH WATER MARK)* – A type of term end point structure that uses the highest anniversary index level as the end point. Say that the index value was at 100 on the first day of the period, reached a value of 160 at the end of a contract year during the period, and ended the period at 150. A term high point method would use the 160 value – the highest contract anniversary point reached during the period, as the end point and the gross index gain would be 60 percent (160-100/100). The company would then apply a participation rate to the gain.

TERM YIELD SPREAD – A type of term end point structure which calculates the total index gain for a period, computes the annual compound rate of return, deducts a yield spread from the annual rate of return and then recalculates the total index gain for the period based on the net annual rate. Say that an index increased from 100 to 200 by the end of a nine year period. This is the equivalent of an 8 percent compound annual interest rate. If the annuity had a 2 percent term yield spread this would be deducted from the annual interest rate (8 percent-2 percent) and the net rate would be credited to the contract (6 percent) for each of the nine years. Total index gain may also be computed by using the highest anniversary index level as the end point.

VARIABLE ANNUITY – A contract issued by an insurance company offering separate accounts invested in a wide variety of stocks and/or bonds. The investment risk is borne by the annuity owner. Variable annuities are considered securities and require appropriate securities registration.

1035 EXCHANGE – The 1035 exchange refers to the section of tax code that allows annuity owners the flexibility to exchange one annuity for another without incurring any immediate tax liabilities. This action is most often utilized when an annuity holder decides they want to upgrade an annuity to a more favorable one, but they do not want to activate unnecessary tax liabilities that would typically be encountered when surrendering an existing annuity contract.

401(K) ROLLOVER – See <u>IRA Rollover</u>

90166941R00112

Made in the USA
Lexington, KY
08 June 2018